Three plays for Ireland
Northern Star
Heavenly Bodies
Pentecost

Northern Star
Heavenly Bodies
Pentecost

Three plays for Ireland by
Stewart Parker

Oberon Books
London

First published in 1989 by Oberon Books Limited. Reprinted 1995.

Oberon Books Limited
521 Caledonian Road, London N7 9RH

ISBN 1 870259 17 3

Cover design: Andrzej Klimowski

Printed in Great Britain by Antony Rowe Ltd, Chippenham, Wiltshire

For
Lynne Parker

Contents

Introduction

I

Ancestral voices prophesy and bicker, and the ghosts of your own time and birthplace wrestle and dance, in any play you choose to write – but most obviously when it actually is a history play.

The three history plays in this volume were conceived and written, in consecutive order, between 1983 and 1987, as a common enterprise. Trilogy, however, may be too strong a word for them. Triptych has a more pleasing ring: three self-contained groups of figures, from the eighteenth, nineteenth and twentieth centuries respectively, hinged together in a continuing comedy of terrors.

The ancestral wraiths at my own elbow are (amongst other things) Scots-Irish, Northern English, immigrant Huguenot . . . in short the usual Belfast mongrel crew, who have contrived between them to entangle me in the whole Irish-British cat's cradle and thus to bequeath to me a subject for drama which is comprised of multiplying dualities: two islands (the 'British Isles'), two Irelands, two Ulsters, two men fighting over a field.

II

Plays and ghosts have a lot in common. The energy which flows from some intense moment of conflict in a particular time and place seems to activate them both. Plays intend to achieve resolution, however, whilst ghosts appear to be stuck fast in the quest for vengeance. Ghosts are uncompleted souls; witness the Phantom Bride in *Northern Star*, handing on to the Phantom Fiddler in *Heavenly Bodies*, and he in turn to *Pentecost*'s Lily Matthews – in whom the cycle of retribution is in fact finally laid to rest, in the only way I can foresee as having any possible meaning.

III

So far as the 'real' characters are concerned, they have been drawn from the marginalia of the historical record rather than its main plot. Henry Joy McCracken was a minor figure in the '98 Rising in Ireland; not enough is known about him. Dion Boucicault was unarguably a major force in the Victorian theatre, but then that is a period of drama which is in itself considered marginal nowadays; rather more than enough is known about him. McCracken's mistress, Mary Bodle, is so obscure that her name might well have been Boall. Boucicault's Mephistophelean sparring partner, Johnny Patterson, survives

precariously as a name on fading sheet-music covers. He did certainly write
"The Garden Where the Praties Grow", as well as "The Hat My Father Wore"
(which, suitably altered, was to be taken over as the favourite anthem of
Orangeism) . . . and also, incidentally, "The Stone Outside Dan Murphy's Door",
a record of which was the most cherished offering on my grandfather Jimmy
Lynas's old wind-up gramophone. Harold Wilson, whose recorded voice is
briefly heard in the third play, was Prime Minister of the United Kingdom of
Great Britain and Northern Ireland in the years 1964–70 and 1974–76.

IV

The first play employs pastiche as a strategy, and the second one a kind of
collage; the third play is written in a form of heightened realism. This seemed
most appropriate for my own generation, finally making its own scruffy way
onto the stage of history and from thence into the future tense, in this
climactic piece.

Stewart Parker

Northern Star

Northern Star was first performed in the Lyric Players' Theatre, Belfast, on 7 November 1984 with the following cast:

Henry Joy McCracken	Gerard McSorley
Mary Bodle	Emer Gillespie
Phantom Bride; Belle Martin; Cecily Hamill	Mary Jackson
Peggy Barclay; Mary-Anne McCracken	Marcella Riordan
Thomas Russell; Second Orangeman;	
Sergeant of Dragoons; Gorman; Shanaghan	John Hewitt
Samuel Neilson; Captain of Dragoons; Teeling	Liam O'Callaghan
Jimmy Hope	Louis Rolston
Patrick Hamill; Wolfe Tone; McFadden;	
Warden; Interrogator	Paddy Scully
Girvan; Edward Bunting; Haslett	Mark Mulholland
Musician	Sean Corcoran

Director   Peter Farago
Design   Joe Vanek
Lighting Design   Trevor Dawson

Editor's note: This play is written in the style of various great Irish playwrights. The manner of writing and punctuation varies accordingly.

Act 1

[*Ireland, the continuous past*]

[*A farm labourer's cottage on the slopes of the Cavehill outside Belfast. The dark ridge of the hill looms up in the background, silhouetted against the cloudy night sky. Behind the clouds is a paper moon*]

[*The cottage is a semi-ruin, half-built and half-derelict. There is a loft and a downstairs room*]

[*The sloping roof is partly thatched over, but most of the rafters are fully exposed: those to stage left are raw and unfinished, whilst the stage right ones are charred and twisted. The end walls of the house offer a similar contrast: the stage right gable is a jagged, crumbling ruin, whilst the stage left one is half-built, with neatly stepped stones*]

[*We are looking at the cottage interior as though from the exposed rear aspect. The loft floor extends towards us for only about half the depth of the building, with crude wooden stairs as its centre edge, leading down into the main room. There is a bed on one side of the loft, and a child's crib on the other. A length of rope is coiled round the massive main roof beam, just above the stair well*]

[*At ground level there is, upstage, the interior front wall of the cottage, with the door centre and small windows on either side. The fireplace is in the stage right gable, and a box bed, curtained over, in the stage left one. The furniture is sparse and battered – kitchen table and chairs, a sideboard, shelves with jugs and tankards*]

[*The entire structure occupies virtually all of the stage's height and width; but it stops short of the whole depth. There is a shallow forestage area outside of its confines*]

[*A lambeg drum and a bodhran are placed down left on this forestage. These drums are played by members of the company, who may each play several roles in the action. A change of role may be accomplished merely by a change of hat, coat or wig, in a style which reflect the deliberate anachronisms and historical shifts of the successive scenes*]

[*Darkness*]

[MARY BODLE *quietly crooning a lullaby*]

Mary   [*Singing*]
I have seen a lark over high Ardmore,
Heard his song up in the blue –
I've heard the Blackbird pipe his notes,
The thrush and the linnet too . . .

[*The moon comes out*]

[*In its spectral light,* MARY BODLE *can be seen by the crib, gently rocking it, and* HENRY JOY MCCRACKEN *can be seen lying on the bed, dressed only in his britches*]

Mary   [*Singing*]
. . . but there's none of them can sing so sweet,
My singing bird, as you,
Ah-ah-ah ah-ah
Ah-ah-ah ah-ah,
My singing bird, as you . . .

[MCCRACKEN *lights a candle by the bed. He carries it across to examine the rope coiled on the beam*]

Mary   [*Singing*]
. . . If I could lure my singing bird
From his own cosy nest,
If I could catch my singing bird,
I would warm him on my breast –
For there's none of them can sing so sweet,
My singing bird, as you . . .

[MCCRACKEN *sets the candle on the ground. He ties a noose on the frayed end of the rope dangling from the beam*]

[MARY *continues to sing quietly, as he speaks*]

McCracken   'Twas the night before Harry was stretched. And the boys they all paid him a visit.

[*Stepping forward*] Citizens of Belfast, the story so far. I stand here before you on the gallows tree, condemned to die for your sake.

I stand guilty of nurturing a brotherhood of affection between the Catholics of this town and my fellow Protestants.

I stand guilty of cherishing the future happiness of our country above that of my insignificant self.

I go willingly to my death in the true faith of a Presbyterian, confident in the blind belief that you will all unite together in freedom this week next week sometime never and I hope you folk at the back can hear me, then and not till then let my autograph be given, R.I.P., no flowers at the house please, notice the rope, by the way, best quality sisal, sixpence the yard, from my father's own ropeworks, orders to be taken immediately following the execution, thanks for nothing.

Mary [*She has stopped singing*] Quit it, Harry.

McCracken It's the famous last words, you can see I need the practice. Imagine standing there mumbling, Would you mind if I just glanced over my notes, I won't be a minute.

Mary So you actually <u>want</u> to be hung, is that it?

McCracken Why, do you think they offer you a range of alternatives – a brand new eiderdown, or a holiday for two in the Isle of Man?

Mary Well, just you practise away at the brave crack, I'm away to bed.

McCracken Is the child asleep yet?

Mary She's dead to the world.

McCracken [*Moving across, looking into the crib*] Dead to the world is right. What I wouldn't give to sleep like that . . .

Mary You're still a free man. They haven't caught you.

McCracken Not quite yet.

Mary You've a whole new life ahead of you. Come on to bed, Harry.

McCracken It's a gag to think of this place as a safe house, isn't it? [*Shaking a loose timber*] We're in more danger from the masonry here than we are from the yeomanry, one good belch would bring it down round our ears. I should never have eaten those peas.

Mary Very funny, if it wasn't for the fact that you never touched your supper.

McCracken How did it get like this, was it burnt out? It doesn't even look fully built.

Mary It's not. My cousin O'Keefe was building away at it for himself and his bride-to-be. She came up one morning and found him lying dead – on the floor down there – and the place half-destroyed. The people blamed it on the stones.

McCracken	Stones?
Mary	He'd took stones from the fairy fort on the hill up there, for the building.
McCracken	Oh, I'm with you, the revenge of the little people. Another triumph for the Age of Reason.
Mary	He was a freethinker, O'Keefe. People hated him.
McCracken	Did they now? In that case we can eliminate the fairy folk from the enquiry, I'd say. What happened to the bride-to-be?
Mary	It put her astray. She come up here on the wedding night, in her dress and veil, and hung herself from that rope you've been playing the fool with.

[MCCRACKEN *revises his attitude to the rope*]

McCracken	So. The old refrain. Every joke turning into a nightmare. Every nightmare into a joke. That's an Irish lullaby.
Mary	She's often seen waiting by the door out there. They say any man that looks her straight in the eye is a dead man. Which is why it's a safe house.
McCracken	Protected by the Phantom Bride. So be it. For one last night. That's very quaint. A quaint way to go for the man of Reason.
Mary	Will you quit that wild nonsense, once and for all, you know your sister's coming with documents, by this time tomorrow you could be on the seas to America.
McCracken	They have their exits and their entrances and one man in his time plays many parts, his acts being seven ages. Or in my case, seven years. That's all it's been.
Mary	Some seven years.
McCracken	You've no notion of what it was all about, have you?
Mary	I'm a gamekeeper's daughter, with a bastard child to rear, I've no head on me for all your dreams of glory.
McCracken	There was a new idea, Mary. We thought we were its midwives. What did it mean to be Irish? When you distilled it right down to the raw spirit? It meant to be dispossessed, to live on ground that isn't ours, Protestant, Catholic, Dissenter, the whole motley crew of us, planted together in this soil to which we've no proper title . . .

Mary	I've got no wit for this, Harry.
McCracken	Listen to me! Please. Just this night. Look at me. My great-grandfather Joy was a French Huguenot, my great-grandfather McCracken was a Scottish Covenanter, persecuted, the pair of them, driven here from the shores of home, their home but not my home, because I'm Henry Joy McCracken and here to stay, a natural son of Belfast, as Irish a bastard as all the other incomers, blown into this port by the storm of history, Gaelic or Danish or Anglo-Norman, without distinction, it makes no odds, every mother's son of us children of nature on this sodden glorious patch of earth, unpossessed of deed or inheritance, without distinction, for the only distinction that matters is between the power and the wealth on the one hand and the bent knee on the other, and we all of us suffer the bent knee, every one, and for why? Because the power isn't ours and the wealth isn't ours, they ebb and they flow from another source, always and only the one source, the island of hope and glory across the water . . .
Mary	They let you have your parliament, but that wasn't good enough.
McCracken	One can't let the animals run the zoo. One appoints keepers. Gentlemen of rank and fortune. Chaps like one that one can trust to keep the cages bolted and barred. That was the parliament they let us have. The zoological theory of government. But we preferred the logical one. Irish animals unite. Unite! Let the natural sons come into their inheritance, Catholic Protestant Dissenter, one big mongrel family, that was it. The new idea. And we were meant as its midwives . . . except that we botched the birth, you see, arse over tip, up to our oxters in bright red blood, the misshapen foetus scrabbing feebly away at the face of death, and the mother howling her entrails out, with the ring of logical faces round her, all concerned, all at a loss, mine amongst them, Henry Joy McCracken, fanfare please, Commander-in-Chief of the United Irish Army of the North, brave croppy boys who fear no noise on the green hills of Holy Ireland and we couldn't even capture Antrim, have you ever been to Antrim, I mean it isn't exactly Paris, is it, it's scarcely Boston, it's not quite Philadelphia, is it?
	[MARY *grabs him by the shoulders and shakes him violently*]
Mary	Stop this, stop it, will you just leave it alone?

McCracken	Sure, what's the harm in letting me talk, it's only talk, harmless words. I'm stripped bare of all the rest. All the great performances. The exits and the entrances, it's history now, the seven ages of Harry. I'm down to the bare, harmless words, nothing more. A bit of brave crack. A positively last appearance.
Mary	God, to think of all the times when I could scarcely get a word out of you. Into bed without so much as hello-there. [*He remains lost in thought*] Come on to bed now, love.
McCracken	We botched the birth, Mary. The womb may never come right again. Christ knows what hideous offspring it may bring forth from this day on.
Mary	You know, you should go on the stage, you.
McCracken	Haven't we always been on a stage, in our own eyes? Playing to the gods. History, posterity. A rough, hard audience. Thundering out our appointed parts, the Mudlers' Club, God help us. A bunch of wet-lipped young buckos, plotting how to transform the world from Peggy Barclay's back room. Ballads and toasts, toasts and ballads. Speechifying. Pub talk. Declarations and Resolutions of this, that and the other, I'd no patience with it all, I wanted to be up and doing.
Mary	Don't I know it.
McCracken	Neilson pontificating away at the head of the table, Tommy Russell rhapsodising into his enth pint, Jimmy Hope banging on about his labouring classes . . .
	[*As he speaks, the ghostly figures of* NEILSON, RUSSELL *and* HOPE *glide into the downstairs room and assume the positions he is describing*]
	And where did it all go at the end of the evening? Pissed away into the gutter, flowing away into the night. That was the Mudlers' Club for you, better named than we know then. The Age of Innocence, that was.
Mary	Sure you used to imitate them all for me.
McCracken	Oh, aye. I could always be relied upon for the funny voices. [*In* RUSSELL*'s voice*] "This Year of Our Lord 1791" . . .
Neilson & Hope	Saint Patrick's night!
Russell	Gentlemen, pray arm yourselves.

[*He hands out tankards to* NEILSON *and* RUSSELL, *and pours beer from
a jug for them and himself.* MCCRACKEN *meanwhile leads* MARY *to the
bed with the candle, then blows it out*]

McCracken   One short night. Why does it have to be in July? Why could it
not be a nice long night in December?

Mary   We'd be foundered if it was.

McCracken   We just have to try and lift it altogether out of time!

[*He lifts her in his arms. The bodhran plays softly.* MCCRACKEN
lowers MARY *into the bed, gets in beside her. The moon goes behind a
cloud. Darkness*]

McCracken   No future. No past. Just you and me. This night, Mary. Out of
time.

[*The bodhran plays more urgently. The figure of* THE PHANTOM BRIDE
appears at a downstairs window, peering in. The figures of NEILSON,
RUSSELL *and* HOPE *within are caught motionless in her special light,
holding aloft their tankards*]

[RUSSELL *suddenly raps the table with a gavel. The bodhran stops.* THE
PHANTOM BRIDE *disappears*]

Russell, Neilson & Hope
          Health to the Mudlers!

[*Lights come up on them as they salute with their tankards a large
wooden signboard above the mantelpiece which reads "Mudlers'
Club"*]

Russell   [*With another rap of the gavel*] Begin!

[*They commence a race to drain their tankards dry. From the
downstage shadows, the tavern keeper* PEGGY BARCLAY *emerges on to
the forestage and addresses the house*]

Peggy   Such a night for noise and villainy! An honest man mayn't trust
in his own shadows, i'faith, that he may not. Nay, nor even
in his very dreams, lest he mumble aught in his sleep, for as
the saying is – walls have ears to hear. Never was honest inn-
keeper put upon as I am! A frolic of young bucks carousing
nightly in my tavern; boasting freely of how they will turn out
Grattan's Parliament and plant a true democracy in the land.
And all the while a spying eye at every keyhole. Still they brag,
howso'er I upbraid them for't. There's falsehood in fellowship,
sez I. Charge our glasses, Peggy, sez they. Lackadays, was ever

such times as these? But then the golden age was never the
present one – as the saying is. Howsomever, I have smoked
out one particular scheming miss in my own kitchen, in troth
I have. Tonight will see her treachery amply rewarded, strike
me dead if it don't, the worthless bawd.

Old saws speak truth, and truth's a pointed thing –
She that steals honey should beware the sting!

[*She slips back into the shadows, as* RUSSELL, *finishing his beer first,
bangs the empty tankard down on the table*]

Russell	Done!
Hope	[*Following suit*] Done!
Neilson	[*Coming last*] Undone, the devil take't.
Russell	Last man pays.
Hope	Settle up, honest Samuel.
Neilson	A pox on this thick ale! 'Twere easier supped with a spoon.
Russell	'Tis three parts Lagan mud.
Hope	Much like the brains of her that brewed it, I fear.
Neilson	Hush, she approaches. [*Aside*] With a proverb at the ready, I doubt not.

[PEGGY BARCLAY *enters the room*]

Peggy	Now then, good sirs, I trust you keep well, but then well is that well does, in my estimation.
Neilson	True indeed, Peggy, and you shall do well by us – if you'll fetch us your finest wine.
Peggy	'Faith, Mr Neilson, haven't I a fresh pipe of choice Barcelona, which I did not yet pierce. I have reserved the maidenhead of it for your pleasure.
Neilson	Let it be ravished forthwith. You may lay the deflowering to my account.
Peggy	Presently, but I entreat a word in your ears, good sirs.
Russell	[*Aside*] Oh, Lord, she will moralise us into sobriety. [*Rapping with the gavel*] Mistress Barclay has the floor.
Hope	She has the walls and roof to boot, Thomas.

Peggy   Indeed I do, Mr Hope, and as long as it remain so, you may discourse together as freely as you please. Ale-sellers should not be tale-tellers. But as the saying is – a nudge is as good as a blinker to a dead horse.

Neilson   [*Aside*] 'Sblood – the proverbs grow as muddy as the ale.

Peggy   Malicious tongues may wag. I can vouch for my own in that regard – but I cannot always vouch for others.

[BELLE MARTIN *appears from the bed in the loft, and descends the stairs to the downstairs room, hastily staightening up her blouse and skirt*]

Belle Martin, where have you kept yourself to this o'clock?

Belle   I have been abed, I have a distemper in the gut.

Neilson   With no shortage of bedfellows to account for it, I warrant.

Belle   None of this company has had the honour, I can vouch for that.

Peggy   We'll have no raillery, miss. Fetch more ale for these gentlemen.

Russell   The wine, Peggy, the wine, I beseech you . . .

[*But* BELLE MARTIN *has gone*]

Peggy   Presently, Mr Russell, presently. What I'm advising you of is – a tight mouth traps no flies. Prithee watch your tongues – in your cups – if you catch my drift.

Neilson   Egad, Peggy, thou'rt a wise woman. This room is indeed become an academy of scandal. To think of what McCracken said last night about Lord Killowen! . . . but I dare not whisper it.

Peggy   Oh, 'tis safe enough with me, Mr Neilson.

Neilson   Why, it seems that his lordship owns negro slaves, in Virginia. And these same black slaves have volunteered subscriptions, to a Relief Fund.

Peggy   A Relief Fund? To what end?

Neilson   For the relief of his lordship's Catholic tenants in Westmeath.

Russell   Nay, Samuel, 'tis a brazen lie. His lordship is merely shipping the niggers over here.

Peggy   Over to Ireland? To what end, Mr Russell?

Russell   To educate his Catholics in the art of picking cotton.

Peggy   Fie on you, sirs, you predestinate with me. But be warned –
                   for predestination is the thief of time. As the saying truly is.

                   [BELLE MARTIN *re-enters with the ale and starts to serve it*]

                   You know well that rash ideas have been noised about in this
                   room – aye, and reported too. And here's the lass can tell you
                   how!

                   [*Seizing* BELLE MARTIN *by the ι.rm*]

Belle   [*Struggling*] Leave be, I've said nothing!

Peggy   I found one of your billet-doux to Sovereign Bristow, madam
                   tittle-tattle!

Belle   Leave be, I say, you oul' she-dragon!

                   [*In the struggle, a paper falls from* BELLE MARTIN's *sleeve*]

Russell   [*Stooping to pick it up*] Stay! A purloined paper, if I mistake it
                   not.

Belle   That paper is my business, pray give it over, sir . . . [*Snatching
                   for it*]

Peggy   Not so hasty, madam spy. Your fancy words won't butter no
                   parsimony, not with me.

Russell   Well, well. Here is fine matter indeed. Pray read it to the
                   company, Belle.

Belle   Read it yourself.

Peggy   Do what you're bid, if you hope to 'scape a whipping.

                   [BELLE MARTIN *sullenly takes the paper and reads from it*]

Belle   "Declaration and Resolution of the Society of United Irishmen
                   of Belfast . . . "

Neilson   'Sblood!

Hope   Pray continue, Belle.

Belle   "First Resolved, that the weight of English influence in the
                   government of this country is so great, as to require a cordial
                   union among all the people of Ireland to maintain that balance
                   which is essential to the preservation of our liberties, and the
                   extension of our commerce."

Neilson	Handsomely phrased thus far – if I may say so in all modesty. Although I find the rendition somewhat lacking in spirit. A touch more liveliness, Belle, if you please.
Belle	"Second, that the sole con . . . const . . . "
Russell	Constitutional.
Belle	. . . "constitutional mode by which that influence can be opposed, is by a complete and . . . and . . . "
Hope	Radical.
Belle	. . . "radical reform of the representation of the people in Parliament."
Russell	[*Holding her shoulders, reading over them*] "Third, that no reform is practicable, efficacious or just, which shall not include Irishmen of every religious persuasion."
Hope	So, Belle Martin, what think you of these sentiments?
Belle	The likes of me is not paid to think but to serve.
Peggy	You've been serving two masters, hussy, but you'll not serve no longer in this house, for I'm serving notice on you, here and now.
Russell	Come, Peggy, you deal too harshly. These sentiments are legal – as well as sensible. The wench has served us well by disseminating them round the town.
Neilson	Most true, let us furnish her at once with further copies.
Peggy	Alack, sirs, there's more fish than this in the kettle. She has writ down, I warrant ye, the list of all your secret committee.
Hope	Is that the truth, Belle Martin? Where have you this list?
	[MCCRACKEN *has stolen out of bed and donned a shirt. He appears coming down the stairs, buttoning the shirt up, holding a paper*]
McCracken	'tis well in hand, citizen Hope.
Belle	[*Aside*] Confound him, he has but trifled with me!
Neilson	Zounds, Harry, is that her actual paper?
McCracken	Still warm, Samuel – from where it was worn, close to the heart.
Neilson	Pour the fellow a bumper, Peggy, he has outflanked even your intelligence.

Peggy	In troth, Mr McCracken, but you're a canny man, and as the saying is – the brains don't lie in the beard.
Hope	This stratagem should be a story worth the telling.
McCracken	Nay, Jimmy, the tale of an average fellow home from the wars, nothing more.
Neilson	Methinks 'twas an ambuscade of the country sort.
McCracken	What say you, Belle?
Belle	You have used me ill, but your own day will come, and may hell roast the whole crowd of you!
Peggy	Still your insolent tongue, madam. You're going out on the street where you belong this very minute! Bell, book and baggage!
	[*She marches* BELLE MARTIN *out*]
Russell	[*With a bang of the gavel*] Citizen McCracken, stand forth.
McCracken	Yours to command, citizen chairman.
Russell	Kindly oblige us with a blow-by-blow of this engagement, sir.
McCracken	I own I had first thought of sending in Lieutenant Jimmy Hope here, the drab has always harboured a special fondness for him.
Neilson	'Twould have proved a forlorn Hope, I warrant.
Hope	I plead a wife – fully deployed in arms, on another field.
McCracken	Exemption granted. So, gentlemen, I was obliged myself to launch a single-handed frontal assault.
Russell	It would appear that you soon enough gained the initiative.
McCracken	I attained her breastworks, fired my bastinadoes – and she was quite o'er run.
Neilson	Bravo!
McCracken	With the plunder well stowed, I concluded an equable peace and retired from the field.
Russell	[*A bang of the gavel*] Citizen Mudlers, I give you Mr McCracken's famous victory!
	[*They drink the toast, and grimace at the ale*]

Neilson	Let us trust that you have suffered no lasting injury from the engagement.
McCracken	I can vouchsafe this, Samuel. If I have caught the clap, then in that respect at least Lord Castlereagh and I are brothers in arms.
Russell	My thunder . . . Belle Martin . . . she is become his lordship's whore?
McCracken	He is even now preparing Dublin apartments for her accommodation. I smoked out the very street.
Hope	And this the cur that we fought to get elected, the people's supposed champion, the apostle of reform – who now sets his whore to spy on us!
Russell	A dog in office, without question.
Neilson	So much for the moderate man.
Hope	There is a tyranny in such moderation.
Russell	A pox on all moderation! Send round that ale.
McCracken	Gladly.
Neilson	Castlereagh – 'sblood! The devil take him, and his confounded Northern Whig Club! Swilling down his turtle soup, in between regaling us with his fine hollow toasts!
McCracken	[*Aristocratic voice*] "Gentlemen – pray drink to our Sovereign Lord – the People!"
Neilson	P'shaw!
McCracken	[*Ditto*] "Pray drink to President Washington and the United States of America!"
Russell	I could swear 'twas his very voice.
McCracken	"Pray drink success to the Gallic constitution" – [*Own voice*] so long as it remains safely in France.
Neilson	Enough of that canting Judas. Let us drink good wine to the honest words of Jimmy Hope, from his Volunteer banners. [*Shouting*] Peggy! [*Speaking*] How went it, Jimmy?
Hope	"The Irish Bastille – let us unite to destroy it."
Russell	"Our Gallic brother was born July 14th, 1789 – alas! We are still in Embryo!"

Hope   What I contend is – Castlereagh is the landlords' darling, and Grattan the darling of the merchants. The men of rank and the men of fortune. They contend one with another – but for nothing more than the people's soul, citizens. They may modify abuses, they may enact humane and liberal laws. But they will join forces to cut the tongue from anyone who seeks the freedom of the likes of me – a common weaver. The swinish multitude is what we are to them.

Neilson   They cannot contend forever against half a million Protestant Dissenters, and three million Catholics, Jimmy.

Russell   If the twain but once unite.

Neilson   They shall unite. It is we who shall unite them. Let you weave their raiment, Jimmy, whilst I print their hopes and dreams. Russell's library will educate 'em. And as for McCracken here – he shall woo them into the one bed.

McCracken   Give us a song, Jimmy, before we grow entirely pious.

Russell   Sing us your ditty about Moral Force, pray.

McCracken   'Sdeath, not a pious song, in pity's name.

Neilson   'Tis a good lusty fighting song, sing away, Jimmy.

Hope   [*Sings*]
                     I see an army
                     Of phantom soldiers
                     From servile bondage
                     They seek recourse
                     They bear no muskets
                     They fire no cannon
                     They fly the colours
                     Of Moral Force.

                     [*Music. The other three rise and join in*]

Hope, Neilson, Russell, McCracken
                     [*Sing*]
                     We wear no scarlet
                     We sound no trumpet
                     Yet we are warriors
                     Of great resource
                     We know the outcome
                     We march in triumph
                     We are the Army
                     Of Moral Force . . .

[NEILSON, RUSSELL *and* HOPE *move off*]

[MCCRACKEN *seats himself half-way up the stairs. The music comes to an end*]

McCracken	Night before Harry was stretched. Boys they all paid him a visit . . .
Mary	[*Stirring in bed*] Harry . . . . ?
McCracken	Moral Force. Couldn't miss. We had it taped. All of seven ages ago. Seven ages of Harry. That was the first age, you see. Childhood. The Age of Innocence.
Mary	Harry, where are you? [*Getting out of bed*] Are you all right, did you have a dream?
McCracken	I did have a dream, days ago, the last time I slept, it was, yes. I was walking alone into town in the broad moonlight, you see, the streets bright as day and deserted except for a roan stallion astray its hooves echoing off the silent walls like gunfire . . . down past our house in Rosemary Lane to Bridge Street. This week they've hung two of my men from Antrim . . . James Dickey the Crumlin lawyer and John Storey the printer of the *Northern Star*, along with two of the Ballynahinch men . . . the heads have all been hacked off and impaled on spikes up on the Market House. I turned up High Street led by the stallion. The four severed heads were staring down at me as I approached, the eyes bulging out the hair stirring in the wind. I stood in the middle of High Street in the broad moonlight transfixed by their gaze my own eyes wouldn't close I felt tears on my face I brushed them away they were blood-red the heads slowly started to laugh they laughed and laughed and then the laugh turned into a howl I covered my ears but the howling was from my own head . . .
Mary	[*Coming to him*] A nightmare, love, that's all it was!
McCracken	A nightmare, sure enough. It'll turn into a joke soon.
Mary	A strong punch is what you need. You've got to get some sleep, Harry.
McCracken	No sleep, not before time. There's six more ages to straighten out. That's first. I'll be sleeping for long enough soon.
Mary	No more of that talk, I won't have it!
McCracken	I led an army of men into a charnel house the other week, so what'll it be, the price of bread, the shocking weather we've been having?

Mary	With or without you they would have marched, to exactly the same tune. It's done with. You've a life to live.
McCracken	There was a man joined us just this morning, on the far side of the hill, Mary. He went through Antrim after the battle was over. He saw a dead-cart piled high with bodies, it was halted by a yeomanry captain. The captain asked the burial party, where the devil did these vermin come from? One of the mangled corpses on the cart raises his head and says, "I come frae Ballyboley". Nightmare turns to joke. They all roared themselves silly. Then they buried him along with the rest.
Mary	So you thought they'd kiss and make up?
McCracken	What do I know about soldiering? A moonstruck linen merchant. All I saw was my own life, as a forfeit, willingly offered.
Mary	Well, you were let off, free of charge. A gift from God, you should cherish it.
McCracken	One last night with you, Mary. That's the gift I cherish.
Mary	One night won't do. You're not yet thirty-one years old, our Lord himself did better than that. You've been four weeks on the run, you're done in and you need your sleep. I'm away to my da's house to mix you a draught.
McCracken	Leave it, Mary, in God's name, don't squander the time. It's not sleep I want. It's your thighs round me.
Mary	I won't fornicate with a ghost – with a man on a dead-cart. The country's full enough of them, I want the man I loved, Harry. The man who gave me that child. You'll have the means of your own deliverance, as soon as your sister comes. For the time being you need your sleep. [*Putting on a shawl*] I'm away to fetch the punch. [*Going to the front door*] Keep an eye on her, I won't be long.

[*She exits through the door*]

[MCCRACKEN *stands by the crib*]

McCracken	So what do you think, Maria? What do you make of your fathead of a da? A long shadow in the moonlight . . . that's about it for you . . . except you'll have to live your life in that shadow, God love you, Harry's little indiscretion, as opposed to all his big ones . . . like his quaint notion of roaming round the countryside, hell bent on uniting together the Prods and

the Papes. On account of how they were slaughtering each other in gangs, you see. The Peep O'Day Boys versus the gallant Defenders.

[*Moving to head of stairs*]

Harry Steps In. A popular melodrama. Scene – the county of Armagh. Nature has lavished its bounty. But civil strife rends asunder the peaceful rustic Eden. Enter the noble and fearless young McCracken – uniting the rabble in a common love for his shining youthful ardour. Music, please.

[*Melodrama music from off.* MCCRACKEN *descends the stairs*]

[PATRICK HAMILL, *clutching a sheaf of papers, steals on to the forestage*]

Hamill	Hist! Who comes hence to my humble cabin with such despatch? Is it friend or foe?
McCracken	Peace, good fellow. I am Henry Joy McCracken, come to assist as best I may in your hour of tribulation.
Hamill	May heaven smile upon your honour!
McCracken	You are Patrick Hamill of Loughgall?
Hamill	That I am, sir, and you're more than welcome to my humble abode, for all the brave work you've been doing on our poor account.

[*Music stops*]

McCracken	What papers have you there, Patrick? Have you the deposition you made to Mr Grier, the magistrate?
Hamill	That I have indeed, sir, bless you. He enquired first if I was of the Popish faith and I answered yes, "well then", sez he, "you are well known in this district to be croppy renegades, and you will pay the price on this circuit at any rate, case dismissed".
McCracken	[*Aside*] Infamous scoundrel. [*To* HAMILL.] So the mutilation of your livestock and the insults offered to your wife, these were not even admitted by him as evidence?
Hamill	Bless you, sir, that they were not.
McCracken	Patrick, a word with you. Mr Cuthbert and I are engaged in contesting such cases as yours. We mean to apply the law against those blackguards who administer it unjustly.

Hamill	An may God reward you for it, sir. D'ye know, I have a cousin wrought for your sister, in the town of Belfast, at the weaving, and she had the highest regard for all your connection.
McCracken	Indeed, my sister Mary-Anne is universally beloved. Now then, show me your papers. [*Taking them*] Before we can proceed in a case, we have to be certain sure that all that was told unto us is the whole truth of the matter.
Hamill	That you do, sir, indeed.
McCracken	[*Leafing through the papers*] What's this?
Hamill	Oh, that was posted on the door there, just yesterday night.
McCracken	[*Reading*] "Go to Hell – Connaught Wouldn't Have You – Fire and Faggot!" Did the Peep O'Day boys do this?
Hamill	Saving your grace, it's no longer the Peep O'Day Boys they call themselves in this townland. As I hear it.
McCracken	What, then?
Hamill	Why, the Orange Boys.
	[*Music*]
McCracken	Attend me, Patrick – did you ever hear tell of the Society of United Irishmen?
Hamill	D'ye know, I recall Mr Cuthbert mentioning something of the sort, when he was dacent enough to trouble himself with our wee bit of bother.
McCracken	Mr Cuthbert and I are officers in the Society. We abide by a simple creed – there is strength in union, weakness in dissension. It is not the Peep O'Day Boys or the Orange Boys who threaten your livelihood and life. They themselves are your fellow prisoners, in this vast cage that we call a country. It is the landlords and the magistrates – the Mr Griers of this county – the gentlemen of rank and fortune, who deliberately foment this kind of rancour between you and your neighbours, for their own greater security. They are the cruel jailers we must unite to oppose! Do you comprehend me?
Hamill	Say no more, Mr McCracken, for I'm your man, and plenty like me, whenever you care to say the word.
	[*Music stops*]
	[CECILY HAMILL *comes rushing in through the door*]

Cecily	Fly, Pat, fly in heaven's name, they're a-coming for to murder us!
Hamill	Merciful providence! Are they close yet?
Cecily	They're in the loanen!
Hamill	[*Bolting the door*] Mr McCracken, begone, sir, begone! They'll not offer you any insult.
McCracken	Who is it that approaches, Mrs Hamill?
Cecily	'Tis the Orange Boys!

[*Two men in orange sashes and with scarves round their faces have passed the outside of the window*]

[HAMILL *fetches a pike from the inside of the chimney breast. Thundering on the door*]

Girvan	[*From outside door*] Come out of that, you Papist rebel, or we'll fire the house round you!
McCracken	I have a mind to talk with these gentlemen, kindly put up your pike.
Hamill	Divil the talk you'll get from them, it's blood alone they're after.

[MCCRACKEN *moves to the door*]

Cecily	In God's name, sir, don't be letting them in on us!
McCracken	Restrain your fear, good woman. No harm will befall you, on my honour.

[*She falls on her hands and knees, saying her rosary.* MCCRACKEN *unbolts the door and opens it. The two* ORANGEMEN *confront him, holding a scythe and a billhook*]

McCracken	I wish you good morning, gentlemen. And whom do we have the pleasure of addressing?
Girvan	Thrustout and Thrasham, that's the only names you'll be needing to know.
McCracken	Mr Hamill is engaged with me on a legal matter, I feel sure he would be happy to accommodate you at a more convenient time.
Second Orangeman	Let him answer to us now, and his girn of a wife along with him.

[*They push past* MCCRACKEN *into the room, the latter turns on his heel and plucks the scarf from the face of the* FIRST ORANGEMAN, *who rounds upon him, with scythe upraised*]

[MCCRACKEN *forestalls the blow with a firm grip on the raised arm and gazes into* GIRVAN'*s face*]

McCracken   I prefer to talk to a man's face than to his noserag. And here is a face I believe I know. Mr Girvan, is it not, of Richill? I enrolled you as a United man but a month since, Mr Girvan.

[*He releases his grip,* GIRVAN *lowers his scythe*]

Girvan   What odds if you did delude me for a wheen o'days? With all your high-flown blether about tithes and rents and the United cause? There's damn-all call for your Belfast prating and preaching round this parish.

McCracken   If you have grievances to air, then out with them. Mr Hamill is as ready to hear them as I am, I daresay. [*To second* ORANGEMAN] You may put up your weapon, friend.

Girvan   [*Of* HAMILL] This man is a sworn leader of the Defenders in this county.

Hamill   And it pleases your grace, 'tis a confounded lie!

Girvan   The attack on Protestants, at the Diamond, a week gone last Thursday, was his doing.

Hamill   Wasn't I winning hay with Shan Durkin on the very day at issue, and the same man will vouch for it?

Second Orangeman
    Durkin was seen at the Diamond alongside you.

McCracken   Pray, what befell at the Diamond, Mr Girvan?

Girvan   Damnable treachery, that's what. We were met together peaceably and they thought to catch us out with an ambush, but we were too cute for that.

Second Orangeman
    One good skite from us, and they ran for dear life.

Girvan   Not before a good thirty of them were despatched to hell for their pains.

McCracken   Thirty Catholics dead, you say?

Girvan   If not more.

McCracken	I see. And so how many parliamentary votes did you gain? How much land? How many remissions of tithes to your vicar or rents to your landlord? In short – how much power and how much freedom was obtained by these thirty-odd deaths and this glorious and immortal victory?
Girvan	I'll tell you what was gained – the Orange Society. We're organised now, to guard our land and religion and rights against Defender savages the likes of him.
McCracken	Look in the face of this man, who is your neighbour, and tell me truly whether it be the face of a savage, as you say.
Girvan	Go forth and ask Alexander Barclay of Richill the same question. Him and his wife and his thirteen-year-old had their tongues torn out by Defenders, and the wife's body further abused till she died within days of her mutilations. Hamill here can acquaint you further with the details of the case.
Hamill	'Twas no doing of mine or of my connection, as God is my judge.
McCracken	You have magistrates, entirely in your sympathy, to deal with such matters. You cannot pretend that you are defenceless before the law, which certainly is the case with Mr Hamill and his kind.
Girvan	Why must your type always side with the accursed Papist? You're a Presbyterian same as me and him, where's your loyalty?
McCracken	My loyalty is here, Mr Girvan, in this room – but to all of you within it.
	[*Music*]
	The country round here is as lush and lovely as a garden, is it not?
Girvan	What of it?
McCracken	It has riches and rewards a-plenty – more than enough for all like yourselves who labour in it. Tell me, why do you not partake freely of them?
Hamill	Sure, they're not ours to command, Mr McCracken.
McCracken	Ah, But they could and would be, Patrick – if you but cease to rent each other, like caged animals, and join with us, in the true struggle, for our mutual freedom. You know very well there are government agents at large, working to foment

these feuds between you. Be not deluded by them! Every
blow you strike is a self-inflicted wound. Go to your home
now, Mr Girvan, and you, sir, I shall investigate the affair at the
Diamond and report the truth of it to the authorities.

[*Music stops. Pause*]

Girvan   We may go this time – on your warranty – but we mean to be
satisfied in full.

McCracken   I shall call tomorrow on you both and take your affidavits.
Good-day to you, friends. [*Shaking hands with them*] Good-day,
sir.

[*The two* ORANGEMEN *exit through the door*]

Hamill   May the saints preserve your honour, you have saved our two
lives this day.

Cecily   Indeed you have so, and you'll be forever in our prayers.

McCracken Patrick, a word with you. Be honest with me now. Are you in
fact a sworn member of the Defenders?

Hamill   Bless you, sir, but sure all of us are, round these parts.

Cecily   Come quick, Pat.

Hamill   Forgive us, sir.

[*As the lambeg is beaten,* PATRICK *and* CECILY HAMILL *exit*]

[*McCracken ascends the stairs, pauses by the rope. Drum Stops*]

McCracken So much for the second age. Idealism, they call that. Also
known as adolescence. Harry Steps In, and acts his heart out.

Citizens of Belfast – you rehearse all of your chosen parts
and you play them with the utmost zeal – except that maybe
they're really playing you. Think about it. They costume
themselves in your flesh and bones, borrow your voice, strike
your poses, and at the end they move on – [*Clutching the rope*]
and this is where they leave you hanging.

[MARY BODLE *comes in through the front door, followed by* MARY-ANNE
McCracken, who carries two bundles.]

Mary   He's maybe dozed off upstairs.

Mary-Anne We won't waken him, if he has. I'd rather wait.

McCracken Mary-Anne, is that you? [*Running down the stairs*]

Mary-Anne	Harry! [*Embracing him*] Thank God you're safe.
McCracken	It's you I was worried for, I felt sure you'd been lifted on the road.
Mary-Anne	I've been at Mr Bodle's house since early evening. I didn't dare come on up here until now, the whole of the Cavehill is crawling with militia. [*Putting bundles on table*]
McCracken	Sit down by the fire, there's still some heat in the embers.
Mary	I'll put this punch by it, to keep warm. [*Setting jug of punch in the fireplace*]
Mary-Anne	[*Giving her money*] Mary, this is for you.
Mary	Oh no, Miss McCracken, there's no call for that . . .
Mary-Anne	[*Forcing it into her hand*] Not another word. [*To* MCCRACKEN] This is a very brave girl, Harry. Venturing out here with me at this hour of the night . . .
	[*To* MARY] You better run on home now, dear, before your father gets concerned about you.
	[*Awkward pause*]
McCracken	In actual fact . . . Mary has been sort of looking out for me.
Mary-Anne	She has indeed, and so has her whole family.
McCracken	She's been staying here, you see.
	[*Pause*]
Mary-Anne	Oh, right. Yes. Well. In that case.
Mary	I'll be in the loft, Miss McCracken. Give us a shout if there's anything you need.
Mary-Anne	Thank you, Mary.
	[MARY *ascends the stairs to the loft and stretches out on the bed*]
McCracken	I'm well cared for.
Mary-Anne	I can see you are.
McCracken	Although the accommodation is a trifle over-ventilated.
Mary-Anne	It's no fit dwelling for a patriot and a hero, that's for certain.
McCracken	Do you mind? You're talking about a charming rural hideaway. Convenient to town. In a much sought-after area.
Mary-Anne	I knew your spirit wouldn't be broken, they all said you'd be in despair, but I told them . . .

McCracken	Any word of Frank and William?
Mary-Anne	Oh, they're both safe hid, they'll be fine.
McCracken	So what about your mother and father and Margaret and John? Not forgetting the bold Atty Bunting?
Mary-Anne	They're all perfectly well, at home. Except that none of us will sleep easy until you're aboard ship and well away, I've brought all the necessaries . . .
McCracken	Come on, I want to hear all the crack about them.
Mary-Anne	They may not understand the struggle as fully as I do, Harry – all the same, you're more than just a beloved son and brother to them now. They cherish and revere you as a national hero, believe me.
McCracken	Fancy a glass of punch?
Mary-Anne	Not one of them would have had you act differently – not even mother, though she could never bring herself to admit it. Oh, she sent you this, by the way.
	[*Taking a book from one of the bundles*]
	It's Edward Young's *Night Thoughts*, I'm afraid. "Procrastination is the thief of time" and all that.
McCracken	Her favourite book.
Mary-Anne	Ten thousand lines of sanctimonious gush. Spiritual consolation, she calls it. I told her you'd no need of any such nonsense. What's the loss of one battle in the great war for this country's soul? The coming generations will finish what you've started, they'll model themselves on your example . . .
McCracken	Christ forbid, what an example! Pious phrasemaking over a butcher's shambles, valiant defeat, maudlin self-pity – "we wuz robbed!" – defeat! What an example. A septic wound. Let them purge the poison and bury us in lime.
	[*Pause*]
Mary-Anne	You know that won't be history's verdict . . .
McCracken	History's a whore. She rides the winners.
	[*Pause*]
Mary-Anne	You're worn out, Harry. Once you're safe away, you'll be yourself again.
McCracken	[*Gesturing at the bundles*] So who am I meant to be in the meantime?

Mary-Anne	Oh, yes . . . I had your papers made out in the name of Owen Pollock, Master Carpenter. [*Removing them from bundle*] This is all carpenter's gear and tools. What you have to do tomorrow, is make your way to Greencastle, and ask at the quay for a boatman called Brownlow. He'll take you across to the brig the *Benjamin Franklin*, anchored in the Pool of Garmoyle. It's commanded by a Captain Moore, who's an old shipmate of father's. Ready?
McCracken	Right.
Mary-Anne	Name?
McCracken	Pollock. Owen Pollock.
Mary-Anne	Occupation?
McCracken	Carpenter.
Mary-Anne	Occupation?
McCracken	<u>Master</u> carpenter.
Mary-Anne	The boatman?
McCracken	Brownlow. The Pool of Garmoyle. The *Benjamin Franklin*. Captain Moore. Philadelphia, here I come.
Mary-Anne	Well done.
McCracken	If only <u>you</u> had led the Rising, we would have walked it.
Mary-Anne	Don't poke fun at me, Harry.
McCracken	I was never more serious. How have you been anyway, Mary-Anne?
Mary-Anne	Oh, you know. Sit at home. Mind the business. That's all that's allowed me, I can do nothing, there's nothing at all I can make happen.
McCracken	[*Gesturing at bundles*] What do you call this?
Mary-Anne	Did you hear any accounts of the battle at Ballynahinch?
McCracken	I heard the result. That was enough.
Mary-Anne	They found the body of a young girl on the battlefield. Her brother and her lover were comrades in arms, on the rebel side. She couldn't bear the thought of losing them both. So she upped and fought alongside them. When the retreat came, the girl couldn't keep up with her two men. So they insisted on staying behind with her . . . all three were slaughtered,

of course. Highly romantic. There were two other female corpses found, standard bearers. Dolled up in green satin as the Goddess of Liberty and the Goddess of Reason. They turned out to be the town whores.

McCracken   That'll please the government.

Mary-Anne   So when the big issues come to be decided, you see, we get cast in the same old roles again. Mothers, wives and mistresses. Goddesses, whores and sisters. Trophies and symbols. The Shan Van Vocht and Roisin Dubh. I presume you love that girl up there?

McCracken   I'm afraid I do.

Mary-Anne   [*Rising*] It's time I went.

McCracken   What do you mean? You've scarcely arrived.

Mary-Anne   If I return to David Bodle's house, I can set out for the coast road at first light, and pick up the Belfast coach.

McCracken   You've been the best friend in the world to me, Mary-Anne. From the very beginning.

Mary-Anne   It would ill become me, then, to add to your troubles at this stage.

McCracken   There's nobody I'd sooner have beside me, in a tight corner.

Mary-Anne   As you say – you're well cared for. [*Moving to door*] I'll not sleep easy till I know that ship has sailed, with you on it.

McCracken   Tell me about Atty Bunting. Is he still collecting away at his folk tunes through all this?

Mary-Anne   You know Atty. Harps on the brain. Harps and organs.

McCracken   Give him my love.

Mary-Anne   [*Embracing him*] Oh, Harry!

McCracken   What a sister. Better than I deserve.

Mary-Anne   Don't! We'll talk it all through, in years to come. Not now. Action now, that's what counts. Move carefully.

McCracken   You too.

Mary-Anne   Goodbye.

[*She leaves quickly through the door*]

McCracken   [*As she goes*] Goodbye, Mary-Anne.

[He leans back with a deep sigh of relief against the closed door]

McCracken   I have observed . . . that a man is never less true to himself than in the presence of his own family. *[He laughs softly]*

Atty Bunting, his words. The words of the foster son. As touchy as he's clever. With his ancient music of Gaelic Ireland, God love him.
Like pins and needles falling into a basin.

[Harp music from off. It continues softly right through the following scene]

The Belfast Harp Festival, famous in myth and legend. Forging a national consciousness, we'd got very keen on that by then. A new culture from the old . . . renaissance!
That was the third age.
The smart talk. The Age of Cleverness.

[ATTY BUNTING enters from the same side as the sound of the harp music]

Bunting   May I enquire as to what you are doing here?

McCracken   I perceive that you are anxious to explain it to me. By all means do so.

Bunting   Very well. You are standing outside a musical recital talking to yourself. That is not customary in polite society. It is a position reserved for beggars and newspaper critics.

McCracken   My dear Bunting. It is torment enough to have to listen to the tinkling of your harps – without the additional penance of gazing upon your harpists. Until I saw the Irish harpists, I was at a loss as to what the Irish beggars did with their cast-off clothes.

Bunting   Fortunately, they are not required to return the compliment – being for the most part blind. Furthermore, a white waistcoat and a velvet cuff are not indispensable to good musicianship. However obligatory they may be to your amateur warmongering.

McCracken   You appear anxious to provoke a quarrel with me. I do hope it will lead to violence.

Bunting   I abhor violence – apart from that which is perpetrated by armed men against people whom I dislike.'

McCracken   Do you dislike the whole of Belfast society, in that case?

Bunting   Only from time to time. On Thursdays they are tolerable
                   enough. I abominate them on Sunday afternoons, however.
                   Why do you ask, pray?

McCracken   Twelve harps strung with wire is violence enough, I venture
                   to suggest. Particularly after two entire days of listening to
                   them.

Bunting   The preservation of the ancient music of Ireland is a noble and
                   edifying task. It is profoundly irresponsible of you to expect
                   enjoyment from it.

McCracken   To enjoy the things that are good for us would certainly
                   transform society. It could even be the start of civilised life as
                   we know it.

                   [WOLFE TONE *enters*]

Tone   I perceive that I have interrupted your moralising, gentlemen.
                   I do hope that the damage is irreparable.

McCracken   My dear Tone – no conversation is ever quite complete until
                   you have interrupted it. Are you two gentlemen acquainted?

Bunting   I don't believe I have had the displeasure.

McCracken   Then may I present to you the celebrated Mr Wolfe Tone from
                   Dublin?

Bunting   Tone, did you say? Musical by name, but not, it would seem,
                   by nature.

Tone   I assure you that I esteem the Irish harp above all other
                   instruments – at any rate, up until the point when people
                   begin to pluck at it. I take it I have the honour of addressing
                   the distinguished Mr Edward Bunting?

Bunting   At your service, Mr Tone. May I make bold enough to draw
                   attention to the badge of your society of United Irishmen?
                   It consists of this same harp, bearing the motto – "It is new
                   strung and shall be heard". It appears in your case, however,
                   that it shall not in fact be heard after all.

McCracken   That is what vulgar people call hypocrisy. The educated
                   classes refer to it as symbolism.

Tone   You misconstrue our absence from the hall, Mr Bunting. We
                   are conspirators by nature. Conspirators like to listen and
                   hate to be seen. An audience at a musical event has quite the
                   opposite inclination. They go to be seen but never to listen.

So you see McCracken and I may prove your truest supporters after all.

Bunting I am not at all sure that I care for your support. For you the real event of this week is the third anniversary of the Fall of the Bastille. Where the rats released the reptiles from their cages. I speak metaphorically. My metaphor is drawn from zoology.

McCracken Mr Bunting is of the opinion that the revival of its music will alone suffice to save Ireland. In spite of the worst that his harpists have been able to do.

Tone Music is the only art above politics. That is why it is the helpless pawn of politics. The old King George adored Handel. I cannot hold that against Handel. It may be the one value held in common between myself and George the Third.

Bunting Music is only above politics in the way that stars shine above a bog. You would do better, sir, to compare like with like, and say that usury is above politics. Or sodomy perhaps. Or anything else you care to name. For what in the world could be below politics? You will forgive me now, gentlemen, if I return to a better place.

[*He exits*]

Tone What a very disagreeable fellow, I do hope we shall see more of him. He has quite distracted me from my headache.

McCracken My dear Tone. You have drunk yourself into a headache on every single night of your visit here. If you had cultivated the loyalist peasantry as vigorously as you have cultivated your headache – why, you might be closer to that uniting of the whole people of Ireland about which you write with such elegance.

Tone My dear McCracken. I have formulated the ideology of the entire United movement – galvanised my fellow Protestant radicals in the South – and taken control of the leadership of Catholic opinion. I feel it my duty to leave you and your colleagues up here some trifling work of your own to do.

McCracken Most considerate, I'm sure. Still, I daresay we may hope to be attended with some little success . . . having originated the entire movement which you subsequently were enlightened enough to join.

[MARY BODLE *stirs in the bed*]

Mary	Harry?
Tone	As for my headache – it does not in fact proceed from my trifling consumption of liquor. On the contrary. The consumption of liquor is the only decent cure for it. My headache proceeds from all your confounded Ulster bickering. In this town one feels like a cat let loose in the dog kennels. What with that and Mr Bunting's harpists, I intend to seek a cure this very instant.
	[*He exits*]
Mary	Harry?
	[*She comes to the head of the stairs*]
McCracken	As to whether the loyalist peasantry is amenable to cultivation . . .
	[MARY *comes down the stairs to him. The harp music stops*]
Mary	Who were you talking to?
McCracken	What?
Mary	Where's your sister?
McCracken	I was listening to the harp music.
Mary	Harp music? My God, did you think you'd died and gone to heaven or something?
McCracken	He was always great crack, you know.
Mary	Who was?
McCracken	Tone. Him and Russell and Sinclair and me went down to the docks on that visit, to have a look over my da's new ship. It was called the *Hibernia* – but there was a crown painted above the name. He really took a hand out of me about that.
Mary	Did you drink the punch?
McCracken	I forgot about it.
Mary	Sit down there and I'll pour it for you.
	[*She does so*]
McCracken	[*Picking up Young's* Night Thoughts] This is a better sedative than whiskey . . . "Procrastination is the thief of time" . . .
Mary	What are you on about now?

McCracken	It's a poem of over ten thousand lines — and that's the only one that anybody remembers. [*Reading*] "Fate! Drop the curtain — I can lose no more . . . " my mother sent it.
Mary	I dozed off, I didn't realise your sister had left.
McCracken	She went back to your da's. Just as well. I could never have got through the night acting the patriot hero.
Mary	Does she not know about the child?
McCracken	She didn't even know about you until tonight.
Mary	She doesn't approve of me much.
McCracken	She has principles. We're a high-minded sort of family, you see. I had a grandfather, granda Joy, — three weeks before he died, at the age of ninety-three, his leg eaten away with gangrene, he made them carry him on a dog-cart from Randalstown to Antrim.
Mary	What for?
McCracken	To vote in an election. He was a real old campaigner, he'd started the Belfast Newsletter, he'd helped to create the Volunteer movement, he'd seen Grattan's Parliament into office. So there he was, ninety-three and barely alive, being carried towards the polling station. My cousin saw him and ran up to him amazed, and said, "What brought you here, sir?" The old boy just glared back at him and barked out, "The good of my country!"
Mary	So that's where you get it from.
McCracken	The man he voted into office was O'Neill, the great moderate reformer. The same John O'Neill who was killed three weeks ago, in Antrim High Street — struck through the shoulder blades by one of my pikemen. That's the sort of family we are all right.

[*He begins to move restlessly about the room*]

No surrender on principles, not an inch. Which is not an untypical attitude, round these parts.
Battling an argument through to the bitter end. We reached that point in the Society, soon enough. The Age of Dialectic. Tommy Russell standing there with his gavel poised . . .
[*Banging the copy of* Night Thoughts *down on the table*]
Begin!

[*The door is violently burst open and a* SERJEANT OF DRAGOONS *enters, with blackened face, rifle and bayonet at the ready*]

[MARY *screams and leaps up*]

[MCCRACKEN *stays utterly calm and composed*]

Serjeant   Nobody move. I'll have the guts of the first one who moves.

[*He briefly checks out the room for other occupants, then returns to the door and calls through it*]

Only two of them in here, Captain.

[*A* CAPTAIN OF DRAGOONS *saunters in, face also blackened*]

Captain   Very good, sarnt. The men are searching the ditches and trees, so you can proceed with the house.

Serjeant   Right, sir.

[*He begins a methodical search of the room*]

Captain   [*To* MCCRACKEN] Now, my good man. I require to know your name, and your reasons for being in this picturesque ruin.

McCracken   Certainly, Captain. My name is Owen Pollock and I am a master carpenter, employed in the reconstruction of this dwelling.

Captain   It is just gone half past two in the morning.

McCracken   Is it really? I dont carry a timepiece, you see.

Captain   [*Picking up documents on the table*] These will be your papers, I expect.

McCracken   As you say.

Captain   It's deuced accommodating of you to have them so conveniently by.

McCracken   I find it advisable in these times always to be prepared to meet the demands of His Majestys pleasure.

Captain   Do you indeed? No doubt with good reason?

McCracken   As you say. You see, we are not unaccustomed to sudden visits from His Majestys servants, in this vicinity.

Captain   You have remarkably polished speech for a carpenter.

McCracken   Master Carpenter.

Captain   I beg your pardon.

McCracken	I enjoyed the benefits of an enlightened education.
Captain	And where may that have been, pray, the Sorbonne, perhaps?
McCracken	David Mansons school in Belfast. He believed there was a good deal more to learning than the three "r"s.
Captain	I believe that Samuel Neilson and Henry Joy McCracken also ran a school in Belfast, for a spell. They had a novel version of the three "r"s. – Reform. Followed by Repression. Followed by Revolution.
McCracken	Join us in a glass of punch, Captain.
Captain	Thank you, I will. Pray do sit down, madam. What, may I ask, is your purpose in being here?
McCracken	This is my wife, Mary.
Captain	I see. Does she normally accompany you on these nocturnal employments? Perhaps she is a master stonemason?
	[*The* SERJEANT *is now ascending the stairs.* MARY *stands up again*]
Mary	Wait, Serjeant. [*To* CAPTAIN] My child is up there. I should like to be with her while the Serjeant is searching, otherwise she may be frightened.
Captain	[*To* MCCRACKEN] So you transport your child to the place of work as well, Mr Pollock? This is carrying familial devotion to the point of eccentricity.
Mary	You may as well have the truth, Captain.
McCracken	Mary!
Mary	Why go on with this play-acting? [*To* CAPTAIN] Im not his wife.
Captain	Do pray continue. I have believed nothing so far.
Mary	My name is Mary Bodle. My father is a gamekeeper, David Bodle, he lives a mile down the road. He doesn't approve of Mr Pollock . . . Mr Pollock has been my lover these three years past. The fact is . . . you have surprised us in the very act of eloping. We were to be collected from here at midnight by my cousin O'Keefe, who offered to take us to Donaghadee, where we can catch a packet for Scotland tomorrow morning. Something must have happened to delay my cousin, but I know he will come. Fate has thrown us upon your mercy, Captain. You have three innocent lives at your disposal. I beg you to spare us, if only for the childs sake.

[*Pause*]

Captain   I am much affected by your plight, ma'am. I freely confess that I have not been so entertained since the last time I was in the theatre.

Serjeant!

Serjeant   Sir.

Captain   Allow Miss Bodle to go ahead of you into the roof space.

Serjeant   Yes, sir.

[MARY *goes up the stairs in front of the* SERJEANT, *and stays seated by the crib, while he searches the loft*]

Captain   Your good health, Mr Pollock.

McCracken   And yours, Captain.

Captain   This Mr Bodle perplexes me. Why would he reject such a resourceful fellow as yourself for a son-in-law?

McCracken   You do me an honour, Captain, but the truth of it is – I am a Dissenter, and Marys family is Catholic.

Captain   They are a desperate breed, these Catholics, are they not?

McCracken   We live in desperate times, do we not?

Captain   Theyve been slaughtering innocent Protestants down in Wexford, or perhaps you havent yet heard?

McCracken   You hear so many things.

Captain   Just last month, it was. They put to the torch a barn in Scullabogue, in which they incinerated three hundred Protestant men, women and children. Entire families. In the name of the United Irish nation. Are you a believer in the Irish nation, Mr Pollock?

McCracken   I hope and believe that Im a patriotic man.

Captain   And what do you expect me to think of that little speech?

McCracken   I never expect a soldier to think, Captain.

Captain   [*Enjoying himself immensely*] Nor should you. Nonetheless – I also hope and believe that Im a patriotic man. Why else would I serve my country? Which country do you think I serve, by the way?

McCracken   You wear the English colours.

Captain   Wrong. Not so. I serve the King, Lords and Commons . . .
of Ireland. King George the Third of Ireland and his elected
Dublin parliament. As does my company out there in those
dark, murderous fields. And every man jack of them is a
Catholic peasant from Kerry.

McCracken   A desperate breed. Just as you say.

Captain   Questions of guilt or innocence never detain them overmuch.
They like to flog a suspect till they can see his inner organs.

McCracken   Your own position at their head, Captain, doesnt sound
entirely enviable.

Captain   I freely own I would much prefer to be in the field against
the French. War is bestial, of course. We all agree on that. We
still seem to admire the rank and medals which it confers,
however. And there are precious few of either to be won in a
civil war.

McCracken   You consider this a civil war?

Captain   The whole history of Ireland is a civil war. It was very comical
of these Scotch-Presbyterian drapers and linen merchants
to imagine they could make it otherwise. There has never
been the least vestige of a nation-state on this island. Nor
will be. There have been petty fiefdoms, Gaelic provinces,
clan territories, tribal settlements – all of them in a perpetual
flux of slander and slaughter. Only one allegiance has ever
succeeded in uniting a majority of them – the allegiance to
the British crown. Now these United Irishmen have divided
them even on that score. It was a dismal farce, was it not? –
to behold these high-minded provincial tradesmen – all got
up like knights-errant in a stage pageant – leading an alehouse
rabble against the professional army of their own countrymen.
How could sober citizens the like of those so grotesquely
delude themselves, do you suppose – Mr Pollock?

McCracken   My enemys enemy is my friend. Perhaps they believed in that
old saying.

Captain   You allude to the French. The French were profoundly
embarrassed by it all, and greatly relieved that they never did
succeed in the attempted invasion.

McCracken   You seem remarkably well briefed, Captain.

Captain   We had first-rate intelligence at every level of the conspiracy.
I see youre a reading man, Mr Pollock.

McCracken	A little poetry is good for the soul.
Captain	I expect you know that bookseller in Bridge Street, what the devils his name?
McCracken	It escapes me too for the moment. Although I have passed his sign often enough.
Captain	John Hughes, is it not? He was a member of the famous Mudlers Club.
McCracken	The club was well-named, it would appear.
Captain	John Hughes was our man. Right from the beginning. We knew every move that the Belfast Society made. We knew McCrackens plans, for instance, before he had even reached Antrim.

[*Pause.* MCCRACKEN *smiles*]

McCracken	Youll have him safely locked up by now then, Captain.

[*The* SERJEANT *comes back down the stairs*]

Serjeant	Nothing to report, Captain.
Captain	Very good, Serjeant. Muster the men.
Serjeant	Yes, sir.

[*He goes out through the door*]

Captain	[*Rising*] Now then, Mr Pollock. If you will gather up your possessions, we shall accompany you to the Artillery Barracks.

[*Pause*]

McCracken	Hark ye, Captain – Id as lief stay where I am, if its all one to you.
Captain	Im afraid I have enjoyed our discussion of politics to such a degree, that I feel compelled to continue it, in a less draughty place. Miss Bodle may come too. If you both prove to be the people you say you are, we shall guarantee your safe conduct to Donaghadee. I own I am not yet entirely beyond the reach of romance.

[*The* SERJEANT *bursts in again, very flustered*]

Serjeant	Beg pardon, sir.
Captain	Whats the matter, Serjeant, you look as though youd seen a ghost.

Serjeant	God save us, sir, but I have so!
Captain	What the devil do you mean?
Serjeant	If you please, Captain, theres the ghost of a woman standing at the gate.
Captain	Are you mad?
Serjeant	I struck at her with my bayonet and it went clean through.
Captain	You superstitious baboon, get out there and muster the men!
Serjeant	If you please, Captain, the men are away.
Captain	Theyre what?
Serjeant	The minute they saw her, sir, they took to their heels.
Captain	Get after them, you confounded fool, I ll have you court-martialled for this, come on!

[*He rushes out through the door, followed by the* SERJEANT. MCCRACKEN *laughs*]

[*From outside the closed door, we hear the* CAPTAIN's *death cry*]

[*The child in the crib –* MARIA *– begins to cry*]

[MCCRACKEN *goes to the window to look out*]

[*Upstairs,* MARY BODLE *rockes the crib and begins to sing softly*]

Mary	[*Singing*] It was on the Belfast mountains I heard a maid complain, And she vexed the sweet June evening With her heart-broken strain, Saying woe is me, life's anguish Is more than I can dree, Since Henry Joy McCracken Died on the gallows tree . . .

[MCCRACKEN *moves to centre stage*]

McCracken	Citizens of Belfast . . . I never even bothered taking the Oath till '95. After that, it was in earnest. Reform, we'd tried for. Repression was what we'd got. So the desire was hardening, hardening up. For Revolution.
Mary	[*Singing*] . . . He says, "My love be cheerful For tears and fears are vain,"

He says, "My love be hopeful,
Our land shall rise again",
He kissed me very fondly,
He kissed me three times o'er,
Saying death shall never part us
My love, for evermore . . .

[*The door swings open.* THE PHANTOM BRIDE *stands on the threshold, bathed in light*]

McCracken   [*Raising his right hand*] In the awful presence of God, I, Henry Joy McCracken, do voluntarily declare that I will endeavour to forward a brotherhood of affection, an identity of interests, a communion of rights, and a union of power, among Irishmen of all religious persuasions. I do further declare that neither hopes, fears, rewards, or punishments shall ever induce me directly or indirectly, to inform or give evidence against any member or members of this or similar societies, for any act or expression of theirs done or made individually or collectively in or out of this Society in pursuance of this obligation. This day of our Lord, March 24th, in the year 1795.

[THE PHANTOM BRIDE *crosses the threshold. as the song continues, he turns upstage to face her. She kisses him, and then, with a predatory leap, clamps her bare legs round his waist and her arms round his neck*]

Mary   [*Singing*]
. . . And is it true? I asked her,
Yes, it is true, she said,
For to this heart that loved him
I pressed his gory head,

And each night, pale and trembling
His ghost comes to my side,
My Harry, my dear Harry
Comes back to his waiting bride . . .

[*The moon goes behind a cloud*]

[*Darkness*]

[*End of Act One*]

Act 2

[*Darkness*]

[*The lambeg builds to a crescendo. Stops.* MARY BODLE *cries out. The bodhran sounds more quietly*]

[*The moon comes out*]

[MARY BODLE *is sprawled exhausted across the rumpled bed, in a state of undress.* MCCRACKEN *sits on the side of the bed, equally disarrayed*]

McCracken	I must have hurt you. I didn't mean to.
Mary	It's a wonder we didn't go clean through the floor.
McCracken	It's a tribute to your cousin O'Keefe's workmanship.
Mary	God rest him.
McCracken	Indeed. For all his freethinking. Are you all right?
Mary	We don't hurt that easy. We're a lot tougher than men. [*She touches his shoulder*] What about you? You're shaking like a leaf.
McCracken	The air's a bit chill.
Mary	Put your coat round you. Here.

[*She disentangles a green frock coat from amongst the bedclothes, and drapes it round his shoulders*]

Mary	They'll not be back this way in a hurry, that's for sure.
McCracken	Who won't?
Mary	The army, who do you think? Brute men the like of that, imagine it – bloodshed and butchery every day of their lives – and the sight of O'Keefe's promised bride is enough to reduce them every one to whingeing like wee boys.
McCracken	I could have sworn to God I saw her myself, down there, in the very house.
Mary	Sure why wouldn't you? Isn't it her house?
McCracken	I can't stand my own mind! The one thing I always cherished. The men of Reason, logic and reason, and now I keep seeing the most damnable things, shadows and moonshine, when I most need to be clear and true. What have I to do with ghosts?

Mary   There's no escaping them in this townland. We're well used
                    to the walking dead, we have more spooks than living bodies
                    round these parts. What of it? There's no harm in seeing
                    ghosts. There's just no call to turn into one, before your time.
                    You're still shaking, what is it?

                    [MCCRACKEN *gets up, looks out at the Cavehill*]

McCracken   You can see McArt's Fort now, clear as day. So that's clear
                    enough, at least.

                    [*He paces about restlessly*]

                    It's a curious thing, fear. The soft unbearable spot on a man's
                    soul.

                    Once touch it, and you've got the man's price.

Mary   May God forgive you for saying such a thing.

McCracken   He hardly will, though, he'd need to go into overtime.

Mary   Isn't it fear alone that makes us human? What else do you think
                    I love you for? Your great doings of renown? Let your sister
                    idolise you for that, to me it's just a load of bells ringing . . .

McCracken   It's thought that makes us human, Mary, the power of thought,
                    the power of the mind. To lose that, that's what I fear, the one
                    thing.

Mary   It isn't that at all that you fear, nothing like.

McCracken   You think it was fighting, fighting the battle? That was
                    sheer pleasure, when it came to it. Clear and unreal as that
                    moonlight. After all the months and years of muddling and
                    backstabbing and bitterness and bull, suddenly there we were
                    marching, with an enemy and a goal, a completely absorbing
                    game, played out in a dream, you were both in it and detached
                    from it, watching yourself strike. Fear never came into it, for
                    me.

Mary   Of course not, not with the killing. Why would that frighten
                    you? It's living that you fear. That's the sore spot on your soul.
                    Living the way I do, most people do. Humdrum, ordinary,
                    soon enough forgotten. That's why you're more in love with
                    that rope than you are with me and the child . . .

McCracken   It's not true!

Mary   That's why you accepted the command at a few days' notice,
                    when the sensible men had all gone home for their tea. That's
                    why you took up arms in the first place, when you knew in

your heart it would spread the very disease it was meant to cure. And that's why you'll choose to swing on a scaffold when you could be living a decent ordinary life in a new country.

McCracken   Doing what? Can you honestly see me, in some Main Street in Massachussetts, behind the counter of a draper's shop?

Mary   Why should that scare you? Weren't you forever drinking toasts to the great new American republic?

McCracken   I belong here. Everything I've done has been an affirmation of belonging here. How can I leave now?

Mary   Right enough. Especially with the prospect of a brave and glorious death facing you – dangling from a rope's end, with the shite dribbling out of your britches. I'll not be there, Harry. I hope your sister enjoys it. It's not the worst either. There's what they do to you after you've long gone, that's still to come. And what's done in your name.

McCracken   Why can I not live a free life in my own country?

Mary   Why did you allow yourself to resort to the gun?

[*Pause.* MCCRACKEN *sits down on the top stair*]

McCracken   It was moral force. And then it was physical force. Nobody just suddenly decided that. It was the inescapable logic of events.

Mary   There's always the choice to say no.

McCracken   Saying no is a final exit. You act out your small parts in a huge drama, Mary, but it's not of your own creation. You're acting all along in the dark, no matter how clear it seems at the time. You only have one choice. Either retire from the stage altogether. Or play out all your allotted roles until the curtain falls.

Mary   Aye, that's right. On a stage full of corpses.

[*She begins to make the bed*]

McCracken   It's all I can say.

[*The future ghost of* JIMMY HOPE *enters the downstairs room*]

Hope   It's no more than we both believed, Harry.

McCracken   Jimmy Hope would have told you better. You would have loved Jimmy.

Hope   The condition of the Labouring class was the fundamental question at issue. A man has the natural right to derive a subsistance from the soil in which he invests his labour.

McCracken   I hear you, Jimmy.

Hope   We couldn't reform a system that was rotten at the core. Known activists had been stripped of their livelihoods. William Orr had been hung. We'd been down every road there was and they'd all lead to a dead end. We'd nowhere to go but the whole hog. An independent republic.

McCracken   Most of the men we knew weren't ready to hear you.

Hope   Why wouldn't they be? Weren't they sworn members of the Society?

McCracken   They were merchants first and foremost. Sooner than see their shipping interests threatened, they would have sunk this entire island and every vestige of freedom with it.

Hope   Bad cess to them then, for they're the boys that would put the rope on your neck and on mine too.

McCracken   You're surely not afraid of being hung, Jimmy?

Hope   I ken it's a great honour, but I cannae say I'm dying about it. Any more than you are.

McCracken   [*Turning back towards the rope*] I have no desire to die of sickness.

Mary   That's very noble and generous of you. [*Getting back into the bed*] The love of your family isn't enough. My love isn't enough. You want the love of the whole future world and heaven besides. All right, go ahead, let them love you to death, let them paint you in forty shades of green on some godforsaken gable-end!

          [*She turns her face to the wall*]

McCracken   [*Standing up*] Mary . . .

Hope   Tone went away to America.

McCracken   Had to go. Indicted for high treason.

Hope   You saw him off, I believe.

McCracken   We took him on a final outing. Up the Cavehill. Up there. McArt's Fort.

[THOMAS RUSSELL *appears on the forestage, and surveys the auditorium*]

Russell   Isn't it what I'm telling you, mister honey? The storied Athens of the Northern world spread out beneath your feet and fit for the son of God himself would cast his blessed incarnate being into the radiance of it!

McCracken   The Heroic Age arrived that day. Mad keen to fight now. Pledging ourselves for the first time to the republic of United Irishmen. Playing our hearts out.

Hope   And why wouldn't you?

[WOLFE TONE *appears beside* RUSSELL]

Tone   Hush now, Thomas Russell, with your preachifyin' tongue. Them that knows the spot for their native crib can sooner testify to its true grandeur, and it the birthplace of their natural genius. Henry Joy can tell us the tale, I have no doubt.

McCracken   An August day. Incandescent. Half a dozen of us up there. High as kites.

[SAMUEL NEILSON *joins* RUSSELL *and* TONE]

Neilson   It must be only lofty thoughts do be detaining you on a rare eminence the like of this one, mister honey.

Tone   Isn't it thoughts of our own dear freedom, Samuel Neilson? And the thought that our eyes will never see it, without that England leaves us to our own resources?

Neilson   There's talking.

Russell   She'll never leave this land, I'm thinking, without that we rise up in the red dawn and scatter her scarlet army before us into the foamy tide.

Neilson   And wouldn't we have the right, and the might itself?

Tone   We've been time and again to her front door, with words of reasoning would draw the breath from the philosophers of old. And time and again we've been to her back door, to only beg for a crust in the honeyed words of a decent man of the roads. And haven't we always and ever come away empty-handed, and the murdering red-eyed hounds of the household set upon us to rend us for our pains?

Neilson   There's a pack of curs will run yelping for their kennels, and we but slip the leash of the fabled Hound of Ulster.

Russell	Isn't there a kind of glory now rising up among us, to be surveying with a lordly eye the only wonder of the Northern world, like the saints and heroes of ages past? The blue stretch of Lough Neagh like a wondrous county of heaven itself spread out below us, and the elegant neck of the Belfast Lough yearning forward to offer its wild wide mouth to the sea's turbulent kisses, and the sparkling jewel of a town that's in it, a prize the mighty Bonaparte himself would tremble at, and he weighed down with the world's riches?
Tone	Let it not be the prize of a prince or a queen – let it be the sacred realm of the men of no property, and let all this present company vow that we will not rest until we can call it our own dear republic!
Neilson	There's wishing!
Russell	Is there not a dacent mouthful that a man could drink health to such fine talking, and he drouthy with the climbing?
Neilson	Isn't there a choice jug of poteen, cooling in the spring by the fairy stone, for them as wants a sup?
Tone	Do we repair then to oil the ardour of our red mouths with a supeen, and immortalise the whin-scented air with a gallous vision of the future times!
	[RUSSELL, NEILSON *and* TONE *exit*]
Hope	We hadn't the ghost of a chance. And it takes a ghost from the future times to say as much. It was left too late, Harry.
McCracken	There was a complete chain of military command, right through the North.
Hope	Old maids, the most of them. Cowering under their beds, when it came to the actual killing.
McCracken	I had enrolments of seven thousand Defenders – and that was in Antrim alone.
Hope	How many Protestants had you?
	[*Pause*]
McCracken	Well. There was you and me for a start.
Hope	You and me and a handful like me.
McCracken	There were tens of thousands on the roll, only a year or so ago. There was no telling how many would rise.

Hope	We know now, don't we? One thing's for sure, though, Harry. Without the Protestants of the North, there'll never be a nation. Not without them as a part of it.
McCracken	Not without them at the heart of it, Jimmy. Our own people.
Hope	It's the Orange Society has the most of them now. The land was at the nub of it. They were frightened that if the Republic came, the Papists would reclaim their ancient lands. It's what some Defenders were thinking too.
McCracken	We never somehow allowed for that in the Mudler's Club, did we? If the twain but once unite, it is we who shall unite them, God preserve us. With our innocence and our idealism and our cleverness and our dialectic and our heroism. And all the time the brute fact staring us in the face, only we never looked. A field, with two men fighting over it. Cain and Abel. The bitterest fight in the history of man on this earth. We were city boys. What did we know about two men fighting over a field?
Hope	It's not beyond resolution. If every man was awarded the equal fruits of his labour – from the land that he works.
McCracken	Forget it, Jimmy. They won't listen. Have you ever known them to listen? We got what we deserved. The wild men from the Catholic peasantry – lumped together with a sad rump of bourgeois Presbyterians. The government had it taped. Up to a month before the rising, the magistrates and landlords were attacking the Orange Society as bandits. The next thing you know – they'd taken over the leadership.
Hope	It was a handy weapon against us.
McCracken	All that would have been forgotten – assuming that we'd won. It's not the British crown that the loyalists are loyal to – it's their own best interests. They're no different from the rest of us.
Hope	We hadn't a ghost of a chance. Not as it stood.
	[*Pause*]
McCracken	You fought a brave fight, anyway. The spartan band. The forlorn hope.
Hope	I'm a Templepatrick weaver, and I learnt enough at the reading to read *The Rights of Man*. For the likes of me there's a world to gain, and precious little to lose, Harry.

McCracken	For the likes of me, there's even less to lose. There was a linen mill on the Falls, and a printfield in Cromac Square – both of which I bankrupted. They'll be well rid of me in the family.
Hope	Your sister wouldn't thank you for that.
McCracken	Are you still working for her?
Hope	It's changed now, Harry. She was a lady, Miss Mary-Anne. I'm afraid your brother John's no gentleman, though.
McCracken	He'll be the big tycoon, that one.
Hope	He gave me the sack, Harry. First chance he got. He's running the business now, you see. It's a new age.
McCracken	God Almighty.
Hope	Evil days. Never you fret. The moral force of the labouring class will prevail, whatever comes or goes. [*Standing up*]
McCracken	Don't leave me, Jimmy. There's two more ages of Harry to sort out. Before that rope teaches my neck the weight of my arse.
Hope	Sure, I'm years ahead of you. Nothing I can do for you now, where I am. We'll not meet again now. No place we can meet now, except in the long memory of this town, the long dream.
	[*Pause*]
McCracken	Exemption granted. You may stand down, citizen Hope.
	[HOPE *exits*]
McCracken	The steadfast light, the real Northern Star . . . him. Not me. His was a light that never faltered. Otherwise, it was penny sparklers and a load of damp squibs. Goodnight, Jimmy.
	[*He picks up the* Night Thoughts *and leafs through it as he climbs the stairs to bed*]
	[*He comes across a passage which stops him in his tracks as he reaches the rope*]
McCracken	[*Turning to audience*] Citizens of Belfast . . . [*Reading*] . . .

"Now plots and foul conspiracies awake;
And muffling up their horrors from the moon,
Havock and devastation they prepare,
And kingdoms tott'ring in the field of blood.
Now sons of riot in mid revel rage.
What shall I do? Suppress it? Or proclaim? . . . "

... as if you had a real choice. Once the sons of riot get going, the gallant bold Defenders. We let ourselves get slowly driven into their corner. The age of compromise, the age of finally taking sides. So much for the great revolution of United Irishmen. It comes out looking like just another Catholic riot.

[*He returns to reading the book again*]

"Self-flattered, unexperienced, high in hope,
When young, with sanguine cheer and streamers gay,
We cut our cable, launch into the world,
And fondly dream each wind and star our friend ... "

[GORMAN, *a publican from Dublin, puts his head round the front door*]

Gorman   Will you walk into my parlour, sez the spider to the fly.

[*He crosses to the shelves, takes down a bottle and two glasses from them*]

I'll have no butty of mine skulking round my own front door like a tinker's whelp. Walk in tall and carry yourself like a free man of Dublin's fair city.

[CROAKER MCFADDEN *peers tentatively round the front door*]

McFadden   [*Wheedling*] You're certain herself is not maybe at large about the premises, commander?

Gorman   And what would it signify whether she was or no? Am I to be banjoed in my own snug shebeen by the likes of her? Name your poison, me ould son.

McFadden   [*Entering*] If I've said it before, I'll say it behind, the commander's not your man for easy scarifying, amn't I right?

Gorman   It takes something all right to banjo me.

McFadden   I'll have a ball of malt, so. As long as you have the bottle out.

McCracken   [*Coming down stairs*] Mr Gorman, how are you this weather?

Gorman   You find me as you left me, Mr McCracken, at your service, sir. Might I present to you Lieutenant McFadden, my aide-de-camp and general factotum.

McCracken   How are you, Mr McFadden?

McFadden   Prepared to do or die, friend – to do or die.

Gorman	Mr McFadden has come on a visit here from me own jewel and darlin' Dublin. He knows me from the ould days when half the agents in Dublin town were altogether banjoed in the hunt for me, till I was approaching the dimensions of the Scarlet Pumpernickle hisself.
McFadden	They seek him here – they seek him there – they seek but they do not find.
Gorman	Divil the finding they'll do, a chara, and me snug in my own little shebeen here in the middle of the county of Antrim, far from where they'd think to look.
McCracken	Your message referred to a business matter, Mr Gorman.
Gorman	It did so, Mr McCracken. A class of business you and me are well versed in, and let them as aren't mind their own.

[MCCRACKEN *glances at* MCFADDEN]

	As to Mr McFadden here, he himself is a boney fide sworn Defender and fit to be of our company.
McFadden	Breathes there a man with soul so dead, Who never to himself has said, This is me own, me native land!
Gorman	Pipe down, now, with your versifyin', while Mr McCracken and I proceed with our serious undertakings.
McFadden	Wasn't I on the very point of withdrawing into me own counsel, till the swearing-in was overed with? You have the floor, commander.
McCracken	The swearing-in of what?
Gorman	The matter in hand, Mr McCracken, being the furthering-on of the grand work you've been doing for us Catholic Defenders in this county and others to boot. Notwithstanding which – there being no affiliating litigation betwixt the twain bodies of men – namely the Defenders of the one hand and the United Irishmen of the other – we are conferring upon you a Deputy leadership of the Defenders of this county of Antrim.
McCracken	Spoken from the heart, commander, spoken from the heart.

[GORMAN *glowers at him*]

Gorman	Howsoever – to effectuate this presumption of office – I have first to swear you in to membership of our society – according to the sanctified precepts of the national Catholic Defenders of Ireland.

McCracken	I take it that this is the wish of Mr Magennis?
Gorman	The commandant of the Defenders of this county of Antrim – the said Mr Magennis – has empowered me as an accredible Deputy – to conduct this officiation in his unavoidable absence.
McCracken	Very well. What do I have to do?
Gorman	All that's needful is to give back the answers to me that's writ on this sheet of paper here.

[*Snapping his fingers at* MCFADDEN, *who hands over a tattered sheet of paper, which* GORMAN *presents to* MCCRACKEN]

	Now then, Mr McCracken, friend. "Do you promise to be true to the present Catholic United States of France and Ireland and every other kingdom now in Christianity"?
McCracken	"I do".
Gorman	"What is your designs?"
McCracken	"On freedom".
Gorman	"Where is your designs?"
McCracken	"The foundation of it is grounded upon a rock".
Gorman	"What is the password?"
McCracken	"Eliphismastis".
Gorman	"You are now bound fast in the great brotherhood of Defenders. You will know your brother when he joins two hands backwards on the top of his head, lets on to yawn, then draws his hands down upon his knee or the table. You will answer by drawing the right hand over the forehead and returning it to the back of the left hand."

[GORMAN *and* MCFADDEN *solemnly enact the first sign.* MCCRACKEN *obediently responds with the latter one. The other two shake him vigorously by the hand, and slap him on the back*]

McFadden	Let me shake the fist of a true son of ould Erin, and any bowser that'll not folly suit is me sworn implacable foe, I give fair warning.
Gorman	You're a man of honourable standing, Mr McCracken, and I'm telling you now, with the likes of meself at your shoulder, you'll not be banjoed.

McCracken   I thank you both.

McFadden   By God I can feel the blood of past ages straining at me weskit
                  buttons, till I could step out now this very minute and tear
                  the throats out of any sixteen Orange craw-thumpers with me
                  bare hands, and be back in an hour for further orders!

Gorman   You'll restrain your ardour till the signal's given by those
                  endowed with a superior sense of conducting themselves in
                  military fashion. Once we're fully riz, there'll not be an Orange
                  cur left in the county with a skinful of life-blood to his name.

McFadden   Oh the French are on the say, They'll be here without delay,
                  And the Orange will decay, Says the Shan Van Vocht.

McCracken   No. It must be understood that there is no vendetta against
                  the Orange Society. It's true that many lodges have been
                  formed into companies of yeomen by their landlords. They
                  will be sent against us, just as the Catholic militia are, but all
                  those men are the gulls of history. Our quarrel is not with the
                  puppets, our quarrel is with the puppet-masters who pull the
                  strings. The English landed and mercantile interests. That's the
                  power and the only power which we unite to oppose.

                  [*Pause*]

Gorman   Wasn't I after employing the very self-same form of words
                  as yourself, Mr McCracken, only minutes before your arrival
                  here? Croaker, sez I, if you're after the fellows that's done us
                  the detrimental damage in this country, you need cast your
                  net no further than the English maritime investments.

McFadden   Speaking purely out of me own acquaintance, I'm not afraid
                  to tell whoever's asking, that your Orangeman is as stout a
                  patriot as the next wan, and a sight more honest than plenty of
                  pious Papists I could name.

Gorman   Take up your glass, Mr McCracken, and we'll pour a liberation
                  to the uniting together in your own good person of our noble
                  and edifying institutions.

                  [MCFADDEN *begins to sing*]

McFadden   [*Singing*]
                  Our cause is just, we shall and must,
                  We'll fight and not surrender,
                  To plant the tree of liberty
                  By united bold Defender . . .

[MARY *stirs in the bed*]

Mary   Harry?

Gorman   Mother of God, it's herself back early!

[*He snatches the drink from* MCFADDEN's *hand, and pours it back into the bottle*]

Will you quit the catterwailing and get down out of sight before she's in on us!

McFadden   Hide like a chiselur, is it? Me that's your boney-fide lootenant from the olden days?

Mary   Harry?

Gorman   Do you hear me, man, make yourself scarce before we're banjoed altogether! If she finds you loading into the little store of drink we have left, there'll be a bloody uprising on these very premises!

McFadden   Loading in, is it? Who invited me in?

Gorman   Well, I'm inviting you back out again.

McFadden   You might explain to your gentleman Proddy friend, just what the Dublin agents was after you for, in the olden days – selling horses that never belonged to you . . .

Gorman   You yella-faced prognosticatin' little gobshite, I had papers for every last nag of them!

McFadden   . . . interceptin' the unfortunate creatures on their way to the knacker's yard and trying to pass them off as foxhunters . . .

Gorman   By Jasus, I'll obliterate you, you grubby little tinker's bitch!

[MCFADDEN *runs into the chorus, pursued by* GORMAN. MARY *has got out of bed and come to the head of the stairs*]

Mary   Was I long asleep? Is it nearly dawn?

McCracken   Seven thousand I was promised.

Mary   Seven thousand what?

McCracken   Gallant bold Defenders. Come the day and a hundred-odd turned up.

Mary   Why do you have to keep tormenting yourself? You know the army had them terrorised, in their own homes, long before the rising ever started.

McCracken	That was the only reason I got any of them at all. They told me – we'd rather die like men in battle than be hunted down like beasts of the field.
Mary	You never saw what the army did, you were in prison all during that time. The half-hangings and the pitch cappings. I come up by Muckamore one morning, from the fair. It was a mournful dark mizzly sort of a day, the air was raw. There was a crowd round a cabin where the Monaghan Militia had a man trapped. They'd poured the hot pitch on to his head and set fire to it and shut him in the kitchen with his wife and children. The very minute I drew level, the man appeared up out of his own chimney, he'd scrabbed his way up the inside, he was burning like a torch, and tearing the very scalp off his head, and the molten pitch running down his poor face and him roaring like a wounded heifer, stuck up there with the people all struck dumb watching him, and the soldiers barking away laughing. I put my head down and walked on and tried to rinse it out of my mind, but I'll never lose the sight of it. People can't forget those things.
	[*Pause*]
McCracken	People do forget, though. They forget the facts that don't suit them.
Mary	They forget nothing in this country, not ever.
McCracken	No. It isn't true to say they forget nothing. It's far worse than that. They misremember everything.
	[*Pause*]
	Although whether I'm any different . . . I've somehow got to get it straight. Tonight. Just this once.
Mary	The night's nearly gone.
McCracken	It was a fashionable look amongst our members. Cropping the hair short, like the French Jacobins.
Mary	What of it?
McCracken	What do you think inspired their idea of the pitch cap? You think pictures like that aren't seared into my own eyeballs and a million more as hellish or worse, you think prison was a rest cure?
Mary	I know it wasn't.

McCracken   We had the true faith, you see. Reason. The logical men. History was a dungeon. The people were locked into their separate compounds, full of stench and nightmare. But the dungeons couldn't stand against the force of rationalism. Let the people once unite and we would burst open the doors, and they would flood out into the clean sunlight. Heady stuff. Intoxicating. Certainly I was prepared to die for it – but only in the fight against professional soldiers in the field, that was all that we foresaw. We wouldn't even authorise a single assassination, and still they happened in our name in spite of us . . . so all we've done, you see, is to reinforce the locks, cram the cells fuller than ever of mangled bodies crawling round in their own shite and lunacy, and the cycle just goes on, playing out the same demented comedy of terrors from generation to generation, trapped in the same malignant legend, condemned to re-endure it as if the Anti-Christ who dreamed it up was driven astray in the wits by it and the entire pattern of depravity just goes spinning on out of control, on and on, round and round, till the day the world itself is burst asunder, that's the handsome birthright that we're handing on at the end of all . . .

Mary   What use is this?

McCracken   LISTEN TO ME! Fourteen months I was in Kilmainham Jail. That's where it finally broke down. The great big new idea. It's not a place for heroes, prison. Nobody could ever know . . . [*He seizes her by the hands*] Just listen to this, you've never heard it, any of it. We finally ate of the tree of knowledge. The famous poisoned fruit. It was our last and final age. We introduced each other to it. Shame, Mary . . . [*Leading her down to a kitchen chair*] . . . sit down there. [*She sits*] Castlereagh came up to Belfast, with a couple of other lords of the realm, and arrested the whole lot of us. Except that I was on my way back from a Defenders' meeting in Armagh. So they intercepted me on the road and bundled me off to Dublin. I presumed a trial would follow, but of course it never did. We were held in solitary for a while. And then herded together.

[*The lights have reduced the area round him to a prison cell as he speaks*]

[*The bodhran is beaten, as three other prisoners join him from the chorus –* HENRY HASLETT, CHARLES TEELING *and* JAMES SHANAGHAN]

[MCCRACKEN *stands on a bench looking out at the prison yard.* SHANAGHAN *lies prone.* TEELING *plays patience.* HASLETT *prowls*]

[The bodhran is replaced by loud hammering]

McCracken	There's carpentry for you. You could hang the whole Four Courts from gallows the strength of those.
Teeling	Them carpenters are By Appointment to His Majesty. If you can't expect quality workmanship from the likes of that . . . where can you expect it these days, I ask myself.
McCracken	You could sing that.
Teeling	I often wondered about all that posh food and drink you see in the shop windows, By Appointment to His Majesty. If he appoints to himself all that they're claiming – he must put away a hell of a lot of stuff.
Haslett	Why do you suppose he's so fat and dim-witted?
Teeling	Could he not maybe arrange to send us a parcel of his left-overs?
Haslett	He's not going to send his Gentleman's Relish to the likes of you, Teeling.
McCracken	I met yer man at exercise this morning.
Teeling	Scant use he has of exercise today. He'll get more exercise than he ever wanted jigging at the end of that rope.
McCracken	He was in Belfast working for Charlie Davis the time I was lifted, you know.
Haslett	It's damn-all to do with the movement, he's a petty thief, tried and convicted for robbing the mail.
Teeling	That's correct. He's not like us. He's an ordinary decent criminal.
McCracken	I've only the one regret, he says to me. That I'm to die for a thing I'm ashamed of, instead of for my country's cause.
Teeling	It's all one to the hangman, though, when he slips the noose round yer man's neck.
Haslett	Can you not bloody leave it alone, the pair of you! Is it not enough to be cooped up in the shadow of death without your having to drivel on about a hanging like a pair of oul' spey-wives!
McCracken	Don't worry, I can't see them ever topping you, Haslett, you have too much of a brass neck.

Teeling	You can say this for a hanging – it assists in varying the dull monotony of prison routine.
Haslett	Well, you can comfort yourself with that when you're waiting for your own topping.

[*He hunkers down moodily on the floor, drawing patterns in the dust with his finger*]

[*Pause*]

Teeling	[*Turning over a card*] The Joker. Maybe there'll be a reprieve.
Shanaghan	Have we had breakfast or not?
Haslett	Is this a time to be thinking of food and a man out there waiting to swing?
Shanaghan	I was trying to remember eating it.
Teeling	You needn't bother, they're holding it back till after yer man's kicked off, when nobody'll feel like eating it. They don't want lags with weak stomachs ruining their good carpets.
McCracken	Come you and keep an eye out, Teeling, the legs are going from under me.
Teeling	[*Going to help him down*] Is the oul' rheumatism bad again?
McCracken	Only chronic. [*Getting down with difficulty*]

[TEELING *takes over the look-out.* MCCRACKEN *sits on the bench massaging his legs*]

Teeling	The rope's going up now. It'll not be long

[*Pause*]

Shanaghan	What was his name anyway?
Haslett	Whose name?
Shanaghan	Yer man's?
Haslett	What does it matter?
Shanaghan	I've just been trying to remember.
Haslett	You need seeing to, Shanaghan.

[*A muffled beat starts up on the lambeg*]

Teeling	Here they come now, the Governor and the chaplain, practically racing each other to the scaffold.
McCracken	They'll be wanting their breakfasts.

Teeling   Here's yer man, with two screws leading him.

                  [MCCRACKEN *starts to climb painfully back up on to the bench
                  again*]

McCracken   Is he bearing up?

Haslett   No doubt he's feeling in the pink, apart from the odd twinge in
                  his neck.

Teeling   Holy Christ. He's saluting us.

                  [MCCRACKEN *is up beside* TEELING *now. They respond to yer man with
                  clenched-fist salutes*]

Haslett   What the hell are you at, he's only a thieving wee get out to
                  dignify his own insignificance!

McCracken   Would you have us insult a man's courage facing the rope? By
                  God if you had an ounce of his composure . . .

Teeling   The blindfold's on. They're placing him on the trap. There
                  goes the noose.

                  [*A roll on the drums.* HASLETT *covers his ears. Silence.* TEELING *and*
                  MCCRACKEN *climb slowly down*]

Shanaghan   What is it they call the Governor in here, is it Richardson?

Haslett   Will you shut your hole, you stupid bloody curse-of-God
                  halfwit!

Teeling   [*To* MCCRACKEN] How long would you reckon?

McCracken   He's a bull-necked sort of a sinner. I'd say twenty minutes
                  anyway.

Teeling   They'll let him swing for an hour at least, then.

McCracken   More like two, knowing them. It'll be a late breakfast all right.

                  [*Lambeg beaten hard. Blackout*]

                  [*Lights up on the four of them huddled on the ground and on the
                  bench, wrapped in blankets*]

                  [*The door is unlocked and a* WARDER *enters, carrying a flat copper
                  pail of steaming water and a scrubbing brush*]

Warder   On your feet.

                  [*They stand up listlessly, except for* MCCRACKEN]

                  God, the stench of this cell . . . there's boiling water here and a
                  brush, so get it well mucked out.

Haslett	We appreciate the water, thank you, warden.
Warder	What's ailing you, McCracken?
Teeling	He's been running a fever since Monday, warden, he has the rheumatism all through him.

[*The* WARDER *prods* MCCRACKEN *with his foot*]

Warder	Stand up, man, I'm talking to you.

[MCCRACKEN *struggles painfully to his feet*]

Are you sure you're feeling sorry enough for yourself?

McCracken	Get me a doctor. You've had your sweetener.
Warder	The doctor says he'll see you when you're sick. What the hell's rheumatism, I have it myself right across the small of my back, am I complaining? Anyhow, you'll have room to spread out soon enough, with this pair leaving us.

[*Pause*]

McCracken	Who's leaving?
Warder	The Governor's been seeing deputations. Prisoners' relatives and MPs and bloody Papal Nuncios, for all I know.
McCracken	I wasn't told of this.
Warder	Every man for himself, lad. Your friend Neilson's got his bag packed. Compassionate discharge. Haslett and Teeling here are next.
Teeling	You wouldn't just be codding us, warden?
Warder	Did you ever know me to joke? [*Moving to the door*] I would wish you good riddance. If I didn't think you'd all be back.
Teeling	Was that a joke, warden?

[*There is a full slop pail by the door. The* WARDER *deliberately kicks it over*]

Warder	Oh, dear. How careless of me. Wasn't it lucky I brought you that water?

[*He goes out, locking the door behind him*]

McCracken	What is this?
Teeling	You know what that bastard's like. He's just trifling with us.

McCracken   Has this been going on behind my back?

Haslett   You know as much as we do.

McCracken   We made an agreement. Nobody leaves this place unless we all leave together.

Teeling   Rest easy, Harry. They're only playing games with us.

                 [*Pause*]

Shanaghan   I heard a great yarn in the yard, about . . . you know, whatsisname. When he was on the run in Leitrim. No, no, not Leitrim . . . whatd'yecallit. Roscommon. He was on the run in Roscommon. I think it was Roscommon. It was your man that's always impersonating people. What's his name?

Teeling   McCabe.

Shanaghan   That's it. Yeah. McCabe. His da had that watch-maker's in North Street. Anyway. He was on the run and there was all these Defenders in Roscommon up for trial. So he decided to try and spring them. You know what he did? He dressed up as an English officer and he got that wee man who's the Antrim weaver . . . you know, that's always going on about the labouring class . . . whatsisname . . .

Teeling   Jimmy Hope.

Shanaghan   Yeah, Hope. He got Hope kitted out like an English sergeant, and the pair of them presented themselves at the courthouse in Roscommon and were naturally sat in the best seats in the house. So this Defender called Dry was first in the dock. Guilty, says the judge. Whereupon McCabe gets up and says in his best English accent, M'Lud, I wonder if I might intercede for this unfortunate man?

McCracken   Did Neilson put you up to it?

Haslett   Away to hell.

Shanaghan   The sergeant here and I, sez he, are recruiting for His Majesty. If the prisoner in the dock will agree to enter the king's service for the rest of his natural life, will you release him from the consequences of his evil-doing? By all means, says the judge.

McCracken   The three of you have sold me out.

Teeling   Leave it, Harry, it's not true.

Shanaghan	So whatsisname goes up to the dock and offers this fellow Dry the king's shilling. Dry's mouth falls open, because he suddenly recognises your man, but he gets the hang of the wheeze and joins up. The three of them waltzed out of the court and nobody the wiser. Isn't it rare?
McCracken	United Irishmen indeed – and we don't even keep faith amongst ourselves.
Haslett	We can't put our families in jail too! If they want to agitate to get us out of this hellhole, how are we supposed to stop them?
McCracken	By telling them. Same as I did. My cousin Counsellor Joy is one of the leading advocates in this city, he knows I won't accept favours.
Teeling	You can't blame Sam Neilson's people, Harry. He's the sole support of a wife and three children. His drapery business is closed down, and the presses of the *Northern Star* have been smashed, the man's destitute.
Haslett	He's also seriously ill.
McCracken	Do I look in good health?
Teeling	They'll be letting us all out, I'm certain of it.
McCracken	What's the odds, so long as you're well catered for.
Haslett	In the name of Jesus will you give over? The screw was right, you're a self-pitying, self-righteous face-ache, and I hope to God you rot here while we're safe at home in our beds!
Teeling	Quit it.
McCracken	I don't rank you with the common class of traitor, Haslett. You're just inadequate. You haven't the strength of character to be the least use to anybody, even yourself.
Shanaghan	There was another time he dressed up as a clergyman . . .
Haslett	We've heard it, in the name of sweet Christ, a hundred thousand times, the same half-witted yarns, your mind's going, Shanaghan, can you still grasp that, you're a mental case, you're on your way to the funny farm! [*Shaking him by the hair*]
Teeling	Leave him be.
Haslett	What's it to you?
Teeling	He's doing no harm.

Haslett	Don't you come the parish priest with me, you Papish arse-licker!
McCracken	Now we're seeing the true colours.
Haslett	SHUT YOU THE FUCK UP!

[HASLETT *picks up the copper pan and throws the scalding water in* MCCRACKEN*'s face.* MCCRACKEN *cries out and falls to his knees with his arms over his head*]

Haslett	Mr bloody high and mighty, see how you like this!

[*He beats* MCCRACKEN *savagely with the copper pan.* TEELING *pulls him off*]

Teeling	Quit it, Haslett, quit it!

[*He throws* HASLETT *to the ground, then bends down beside* MCCRACKEN *to minister to his wounds*]

God, you've probably killed him.

[*Pause*]

Shanaghan	You mind Harry dressing up as a clergyman? When he went and talked that character out of turning king's evidence? You know, in the cell down by the sickroom . . . what was his name?

[*The lambeg beaten. Lights out to black*]

[*A white light fades up slowly, directly overhead. The three actors who played* TEELING, HASLETT *and* SHANAGHAN *are standing facing the back wall, leaning on their fingertips, arms akimbo, against the wall, feet splayed out, with hoods over their heads*]

[MCCRACKEN *sits on the bench, facing out front, the blanket draped over his head like a shawl*]

McCracken	Finish soon now, it must be nearly now, never soon enough, for me to finish, to be finished. First the tight collar of hair, the alleged word of God, spoken at you, over your head, even he needs words, vanity of vanities, faces all around below, swarming for the choicest view. All as in a dream, before the other dream unknown, perchance dreamless. Unknown. Then the man of God safely gone, and the faces, and the black hood, waiting, for the sign. So then the plunge, the wrench, the plunge, the rough strangle, and so there an end. To finish. Unless only to begin anew, there is of course that. Only to glimmer on in the effigy of another time, other times, other

effigies, never to know end's mercy, never to be let end, never to know mercy, so much for the rope's comfort, I shall soon be quite enshrined in spite of all. A whore's pox then on the future! And I forgive it nothing, for there's nothing it will learn from those of us who swung for it, no peace to be got from it, for those of us who want nothing more now than to finish, a cat's flux on whatever holy picture they may fashion of me!

[*Deafening "white noise" is heard*]

[*The three hooded prisoners howl.* MCCRACKEN *covers his ears*]

[*An* INTERROGATOR *bursⁱ in carrying a baton. He pulls the first hooded prisoner away from the wall, throws him to the ground, and pinions him across the throat with the baton*]

[*The noise stops*]

[*Rapid crossfire of speech*]

Interrogator	Who commanded the rebels in Down?
Prisoner 1	The Reverend William Steel Dickson.
Interrogator	What happened him?
Prisoner 1	He was arrested on June 4th.
Interrogator	Who took over the command?
Prisoner 1	George Sinclair.
Interrogator	What happened him?
Prisoner 1	He resigned.

[*White noise. The* INTERROGATOR *shoves* PRISONER 1 *offstage, grabs* PRISONER 2 *and thrusts him to the ground in the same manner*]

[*Noise stops*]

Interrogator	Who commanded the rebels in Antrim?
Prisoner 2	Robert Simms.
Interrogator	What happened him?
Prisoner 2	He resigned on June 2nd.
Interrogator	Who was appointed to take over?
Prisoner 2	It was meant to be Henry Monro or John Coulter.
Interrogator	What happened them?
Prisoner 2	They couldn't be found.

[*White noise. The* INTERROGATOR *thrusts* PRISONER 2 *offstage and grabs* PRISONER 3 *as before*]

[*Noise stops*]

Interrogator   Who took over from George Sinclair in Down?

Prisoner 3   Henry Joy McCracken.

Interrogator   Who was given the command in Antrim?

Prisoner 3   Henry Joy McCracken.

Interrogator   Are you trying to take a hand out of me?

Prisoner 3   I swear to God, he was made Commander-in-Chief of the whole Army of the North.

Interrogator   When was he made this Commander-in-Chief?

Prisoner 3   Three days before the rising, that's all. June 4th.

[MCCRACKEN *stands up, throwing off the blanket*]

McCracken   Tomorrow we march on Antrim – drive the garrison of Randalstown before you, and hasten to form a junction with the Commander-in-Chief. The First Year of Liberty, 6 June 1798!

[*White noise*]

[*The* INTERROGATOR *manhandles* PRISONER 3 *offstage leaving* MCCRACKEN *alone, covering his ears*]

[*As the noise stops, the lighting returns to normal, and* MARY BODLE *runs forward to comfort* MCCRACKEN]

[*A blackbird's song is faintly heard, and continues through to the end of the play*]

Mary   Harry! [*She hugs him*]

McCracken   Is it time yet?

Mary   No. No. Not yet.

McCracken   I can hear a blackbird.

Mary   He's singing in his sleep.

McCracken   Three days to forge a nation in. With a couple of thousand men with pikes. One field piece, that fell apart the third time it was fired.

Mary	Hush, love.
McCracken	We actually had the town sewn up, even so. The cavalry were penned in. Then the men from Randalstown arrived, and met the cavalry clattering down towards them in a fast retreat. Except that they mistook it for an attack and ran like the hammers. The panic spread to my men. They ran too. So that was it. We were defeated by the enemy's retreat. It's not often you hear that said.
Mary	Come and lie with me, Harry. There's still time enough. Please.

[*She leads him to the bottom of the stairs. He stops, looks out front*]

McCracken	There's a streak of grey in the sky. Over the town. Look.
Mary	The sun won't be fully up for a good half hour yet.
McCracken	You go on up, Mary, I'll follow you in a minute, I promise.

[*She goes slowly up the stairs, lies down on the bed. He continues staring out front*]

McCracken	Why would one place break your heart, more than another? A place the like of that? Brain-damaged and dangerous, continuously violating itself, a place of perpetual breakdown, incompatible voices, screeching obscenely away through the smoky dark wet. Burnt out and still burning. Nerve-damaged, pitiable. Frightening. As maddening and tiresome as any other pain-obsessed cripple. And yet what would this poor fool not give to be able to walk freely again from Stranmillis down to Ann Street . . . cut through Pottinger's Entry and across the road for a drink in Peggy's . . . to dander on down Waring Street and examine the shipping along the river, and back on up to our old house . . . we can't love it for what it is, only for what it might have been, if we'd got it right, if we'd made it whole. If. It's a ghost town now and always will be, angry and implacable ghosts. Me condemned to be one of their number. We never made a nation. Our brainchild. Stillborn. Our own fault. We botched the birth. So what if the English do bequeath us to one another some day? What then? When there's nobody else to blame except ourselves?

[*He turns and proceeds slowly up the stairs.* MARY *begins to croon, quietly, "My Singing Bird"*]

[*Dawn is breaking*]

McCracken [*By the rope at the top of the stairs*] There is of course another walk through the town still to be taken. From Castle Place to Cornmarket, and down to the Artillery Barracks in Ann Street. And from thence back up Cornmarket to the scaffold. So what am I to say to the swarm of faces?

[*He places the noose round his neck*]

Citizens of Belfast . . .

[*The lambeg is loudly beaten, drowning out any further words: along with the singing of* MARY *and the blackbird*]

[*Fade lights to black*]

[*End*]

Heavenly Bodies

Heavenly Bodies was first performed (in an earlier version) in the Birmingham Repertory Theatre on 21 April 1986 with the following cast:

Dion Boucicault	Timothy Spall
Johnny Patterson	Sam Dale
Drama students and all other parts	Marc Culwick, Marie Francis,
	Iain Glen, Allison Harding,
	Paul Kiernan, Paul Mulrennan,
	Crispin Redman, Hilary Reynolds,
	Devon Scott, Timothy Watson

Director   Peter Farago
Design   Saul Radomsky
Lighting Design   Benny Ball
Costume Design   Ian MacNeil
Composer   Jim Parker
Musical Director   Bryan Bennett

Act 1

[*September 16th, 1890. Morning*]

[*The stage of the Madison Square Theatre, New York City*]

[*The curtain is up and a worklight is on. The stage is bare except for random bits and pieces of scenery and furniture, which the drama students attached to the theatre have commandeered, for use in particular scenes and speeches on which they have been working*]

[*A class is in progress. A student called* THOMAS BELNAP *is declaiming a speech of Faust's from* Faust and Marguerite *by* DION BOUCICAULT]

[BOUCICAULT *himself is the teacher. Three months short of seventy, he sits slumped in a bath-chair, muffled up against the cold and damp in a capacious greatcoat and muffler, with an embroidered smoking hat on his head from which protrude at the sides two tufts of white hair*]

[*A second student, a tall and striking dark-haired girl called* JESSIE MCDERMOT, *sits off to one side, awaiting her turn*]

[*The remaining three (or more) students are in a group on the side opposite to her*]

Belnap	"Oh, philosophic fool! Oh miserable pedant, already old – old without ever having known a human joy or human sympathy!"
Boucicault	Can't hear you.
Belnap	"Old without a happy memory of youth – the tender thought of love –"
Boucicault	For God's sake, boy, speak up.
Belnap	"– the high-souled taste of glory! I will know them yet! I will, if I call unto my aid the Spirit of all evil! The wind rises! The thunder peals! Satan! I invoke thee!"
Boucicault	[*Startlingly loud*] SATAN CANNOT HEAR YOU, MR BELNAP!
Belnap	[*Breaking off*] May I once again point out, sir, that my throat is inflamed and painfully swollen . . .
Boucicault	What do you expect, you've been abusing it all morning, and me along with it. I suggest we both go home and take to our beds.

Belnap	May I take it from that that I am excused class?
Boucicault	Indeed you may, Mr Belnap. [*As* BELNAP *is on the point of leaving*] Don't bother coming back, if you've any sense – except in the unlikely event that you develop a voice one day. [BELNAP *sweeps out*]
Boucicault	The wind rises! The thunder peals! And the small rain down it rains for three godforsaken days now, go home the whole crowd of you, I'm not well enough for this.
Students	[*A chorus of protest*] But sir! But Mr Boucicault! I have a speech by heart! We have a scene prepared! What about the exercises? We have two more hours! etc.
Boucicault	Enough! My head hurts, my arm hurts, I have nothing to teach you, leave me in peace. Disperse to your homes and batten your doors against the rising flood. [*The* STUDENTS *slowly file out.* JESSIE MCDERMOT *being the last in line*]
Boucicault	[*To her*] Not you. [*She turns back, waits*] [BOUCICAULT *sits silent for a moment, turning his eyes up to the roof. The rain can be heard steadily falling on it*]
Boucicault	Listen to it. A flood coming on the land, what does it portend? What is the name of this vile theatre anyway?
Jessie	The Madison Square Theatre, New York City. As you know very well – sir.
Boucicault	Stench. Dank. The sweet, sickly breath of a dark house, I abominate a dark theatre above all things on earth, you have learnt what that means, I hope, to go dark?
Jessie	To close down, Mr Boucicault. No performance.
Boucicault	In which year were you born, Miss McDermot?
Jessie	1868, sir.
Boucicault	I had already been writing plays for thirty years by that time. [*Almost with a sneer*] Just fancy. I do begin to feel it has been too long a jig. I begin to see the pathos of it. Move me into the light. [*She pushes his chair upstage centre*] I trust you brought in news from Ireland to read to me today.
Jessie	There's just one item. An obituary. [*Pulling a magazine from her pocket*]

Boucicault	Not mine, I hope.
Jessie	Hardly.
Boucicault	As a matter of fact, I have always found my previous obituaries very gratifying. The moment they feel assured that you're safely in hell, they'll praise you to high heaven.
Jessie	Johnny Patterson's been killed.
Boucicault	Oh, him.
Jessie	You knew him?
Boucicault	Touched me once for ten guineas, drank it the same night of course, still owes me. The culchie little tinker's get had the temerity to compare himself to me.
Jessie	I guess you don't want to hear this . . .
Boucicault	On the contrary, read it, it will undoubtedly cheer me up.
Jessie	[*Reading*] "Johnny Patterson, the Irish Singing Clown, met his death last week in the circus ring in a most untimely accident. He was a devout patriot of his native Ireland, who nevertheless had come to believe that the one hope for that troubled isle lay in a commingling of the Orange and the Green, an accommodation between the Nationalist and Unionist factions . . . "
Boucicault	You have to be a real clown to believe in that.
Jessie	"To this end he wrote a song, 'Do Your Best For One Another' . . . "
	[BOUCICAULT *gives a derisive laugh*]
Jessie	" . . . which he performed for the first time in the big top of Keely and Patterson's Circus in Tralee on May 27th, holding in one hand a flag showing the harp and in his other, one showing the crown . . . "
Boucicault	Permit me to speculate – abuse hurled from both sides, faction fights ensuing, Patterson set upon by both camps simultaneously.
Jessie	It just says there was a riot, he was trying to save the circus equipment from the mob, and was struck on the head by an iron bar.
Boucicault	Better still. Did he manage an exit line?

Jessie	It doesn't say.
Boucicault	Never knew the meaning of the word exit, the cocksure little scut. No class, you see, no sense of timing. Now when I was starting out in the London theatre, Miss McDermot, there was considered to be only the one correct way to make an exit. You stood up. [*He suddenly and disconcertingly does so*] You walked to the side. [*He does this also*] You had reserved the last words of the scene for this move, you thereupon spoke them – and so off. The older actors were lost otherwise, they used to plead with me – "dear boy, can't you possibly offer me a few words to take me off, you've left me high and dry" . . . [JESSIE *smiles; he approaches her*] You intend to be queen of this castle, don't you, Jessie?
Jessie	I'm here to learn how to act . . .

[*He leads her to the bath-chair as though to a throne, and hands her into it*]

Boucicault	It will not be enough merely to give your body for that crown. [*He crouches over her, fondling her hair and neck*] It demands possession of your immortal soul. [*He suddenly pinions her in the chair, his face close to hers*] Look. Out there. What do you see out there?
Jessie	Let go of me, please.
Boucicault	The jaws of the beast, stretched wide, opening up its huge dark gullet to me, oh not to bite, not any longer, it's merely yawning in my face, can you smell it, the breath? The decomposing carcase in its gut? It will swallow me now without even noticing . . .
Jessie	Stop this stupidness!
Boucicault	[*Breaking away from her*] I have written for a monster who forgets!
Jessie	You are Dion Boucicault, you are hardly likely to let us forget it nor the public either . . . you are the famous Myles-na-Coppaleen and Conn the Shaughraun, as any passer-by will testify, and you damned well know it!

[BOUCICAULT *steps down in front and adopts the demeanour and voice of his character Conn, addressing the audience with the final words of the Shaughraun*]

Boucicault   She says you will go bail for me . . . You are the only friend
                    I have. Long life t'ye! — Many a time have you looked over
                    my faults — will you be blind to them now and hold out your
                    hands once more to a poor Shaughraun?

                    [*And he waits, with winning smile and arms akimbo, for the
                    automatic applause*]

                    [*Silence. He looks round for* JESSIE. *She has slipped away*]

Boucicault   Jessie? Back on stage at once. I want to hear that speech
                    of Marguerite's. Jessie? [*The distant sound of the stage door
                    slamming is heard from off*] NO! [*He rushes offstage in pursuit*]
                    Come back here! How dare you leave me on my own!

                    [*After a moment, he returns to the stage, hunched and frightened-
                    looking — there's nobody left now for whom to perform. Just the
                    dark gullet of the auditorium confronting him. He turns, raises his
                    head, looks right into the blackness of it. With an immense effort,
                    he switches on the charmlight of his stage persona*]

Boucicault   Dear friends, you have shown this poor old actor great
                    kindness, yes indeed you have. May I now humbly offer in
                    return a few lines from a part I composed many years ago, for
                    the illustrious Mr Charles Kean, later to comprise one of the
                    greatest triumphs of my dear good friend Mr Henry Irving . . .
                    and most recently essayed here in the city of New York by
                    your humble servant. From Act Four of my *Louis The Eleventh*
                    — the king addresses his hermit confessor . . .

                    [*As Louis XI*]
                    Oh, could you look into my soul, my father,
                    My body's anguished is but half my pain:
                    The present is a terror, but the past —
                    Oh Heaven I dare not turn and look on that!
                    My days are wretched, yet they bring relief
                    And come to scare away my nights of terror.
                    The gloom takes forms to mock and jibe at me;
                    The silence whispers names I loathe and dread;
                    And when I sleep, a demon sits and broods . . .

                    [*He is beginning to feel dizzy, and tugs at the neck of his greatcoat*]

                    . . . a demon sits and broods
                    Upon my heart . . . a demon sits and broods upon my . . .
                    Upon my heart, I thrust him out . . . I thrust him . . . Jessie . . .
                    somebody? . . . AAAHH! [*He stumbles forward in the throes of a
                    heart attack, trying to tear his coat open, and collapses*]

[*Transformation*]

[*Worklight snapped out, footlights snapped on. music bursting forth*]

[*And the ghost of* JOHNNY PATTERSON *rises up from below the stage in an aureole of smoke*]

[*He is dressed in his Irish Singing Clown outfit: a baggy tweed suit with shamrocks embroidered on the arms and legs, and a harp on the chest, knee-length white stockings, a conical hat, and a handlebar moustache. There is blood on his forehead and shoulder. He is singing*]

Patterson   [*Singing*] As I was climin' one fine Spring mornin'
On high Slieve Gullion and the air so sweet,
I spied above me a poor old woman
With most of Ireland spread at her feet –
Upon that vision she was a-gazin'
Whilst from her eyes there sprang a tear,
Yet could I hear from that wither'd bosom
A young girl's voice proud and clear –

Do your best for one another,
Not for Erin or the Queen;
Make your peace with one another,
Sure we all love our isle of green.
Though my family be divided,
Still this land we all must share,
Do your best for one another –
'Tis your mother's dying prayer!

[*Tenderly, he assists* BOUCICAULT *to arise from the floor. The music turns into a manic jig.* PATTERSON *whirls* BOUCICAULT *around the stage, then drops him into the bath-chair and leans over the back of it looking down at him. The music ends*]

Patterson   There you go, Boosy. That's you warmed up.

Boucicault   What has happened? Am I dead?

Patterson   Now you'd hardly be warmed up if you were dead – would you? Naw, you're only dying, like the rest of the population.

Boucicault   What trick is this?

Patterson   Sure it's only little Johnny Patterson – come to fetch you home for your tea.

[BOUCICAULT *starts up out of the chair, moves to a safe distance*]

Boucicault	That song you were singing . . . was it the one that started the riot in Tralee?
Patterson	It was, to be sure.
Boucicault	No wonder they kicked you to death.
Patterson	See now, you're a born comedian. Paddy the Clown!
Boucicault	What do you want of me?
Patterson	One good clown deserves another. You and me, Boosy . . . we're going where the good Paddies go.

[BOUCICAULT *forcibly wills himself to rise above the occasion*]

Boucicault	Another time, perhaps. I have my best plays in me still. Heaven will have to endure my absence for a little longer.
Patterson	God, but you're a prize turn . . . as if heaven had any interest in the likes of you and me! We're show people, Boosy. Not legitimate. Heaven is for poetasters and verse dramatists, fellows that paint in water-colours – Englishman and suchlike. You wouldn't even like it there.
Boucicault	I am unimpressed by hellfire, if that is what you are now threatening.
Patterson	No fear of that, surely – with your Uncle Charlie a well-connected Church of Ireland minister? No, no . . . it's a dark little limbo that's reserved for you, Boosy. A dark and dacent corner of obscurity . . . altogether removed from off the face of this earth. Time's up, oul' son. You have been sent for.
Boucicault	NO! I am owed a place in posterity!
Patterson	No such thing. It's not in the contract. Your soul's not your own, sure you signed it away to the show business half a century ago.
Boucicault	I was a born poet of Ireland and I devoted my life to the drama!
Patterson	You were born a chancer and you sold your gombeen soul to the highest bidder, now – your three score years and ten are up, your three or four entire fortunes duly made and squandered, your three or four hundred young girls come and gone . . . and the account's being called in. This way please!

[*And he sweeps* BOUCICAULT *across the stage on to the trap, which begins to descend again*]

Patterson   We're going dark for real now, Boosy. Down into the dacent dark, like the faithful clowns we are . . .

Boucicault   WAIT!

[The trap stops in its descent]

Boucicault   I demand the rights of a condemned man. I demand a fair appeal. A review of this case. That is my sacred last wish. [PATTERSON *is unimpressed*] Furthermore . . . I am willing to overlook the ten guineas.

Patterson   *[Shouting off]* All right, bring her back up! *[To himself, as the trap ascends again]* I knew there'd be trouble with this one. *[To* BOUCICAULT*]* Stay there till I tell you. *[He circles round the stage, shouts]* Stand by for a reprise! . . . *[To* BOUCICAULT*]* that's reprise, now, with an "s" . . . I did not say <u>reprieve</u>, in case you're wondering . . . right, here we go. Kettle drums!

[The drums begin a low roll]

Patterson   No, no, hang on a mo. *[The drum roll stops: to* BOUCICAULT*]* How far back are we meant to enquire exactly? Are we start with the actual night you were begot? Speaking of things that aren't legit?

Boucicault   There's no call for that!

Patterson   No, I thought you'd sooner skip that, just as well anyhow, from the management's point of view, right – we'll simply have to take the plunge and hope for the best, here we go. Kettle drums!

[The drum roll starts again]

Patterson   DIONYSIUS . . . LARDNER . . . BOURSIQUOT, wait, wait, hang on just a minute. *[The drum roll stops]* I mean, what the hell class of a name is that? For the son of a liquor merchant in North Dublin?

Boucicault   Dionysius was a Greek god, as it happens . . .

Patterson   . . . and Lardner was a Protestant goat, right?

Boucicault   Dr. Lardner is neither here nor there, I am the son of Samuel Smith Boursiquot . . .

Patterson   You're half a god and half a goat, by the sound of it.

Boucicault   Samuel Smith Boursiquot, who was the descendant of a distinguished line of Huguenot immigrants . . .

Patterson	He was a daft oul' codger, if he couldn't even make a living selling drink to the Irish!
Boucicault	Samuel Smith Boursiquot, who was a purveyor of fine wines in the city of Dublin . . . [*Beginning to step forward*]
Patterson	That'll do! Contain yourself. I haven't got all day, you know.

[*He turns out front again, drawing himself up importantly.*

Right. Here we go. Kettle drums.

[*The drums begin their low roll again*]

Dionysius . . . Lardner . . . Boursiquot . . . [*The drum roll peaks and stops*] This Is Your Life!

[*Blackout*]

[*Raucous circus music*]

[*Flashes of lightning, in which* PATTERSON *is glimpsed, laughing maniacally and tumbling across the stage*]

[*A final flash of lightning and a concluding circus fanfare*]

[*Now there is full blackout and stillness, with only the sound of a distant solo violin playing an elegiac air*]

[*The light of the morning sun comes slowly up on* BOUCICAULT. *His greatcoat, muffler, smoking hat and tufts of white hair are gone. He is instead an elegant young man of the 1850's, rather dandified in his braided frock coat and floppy bow tie and natty waistcoat and trousers. His hair is dark, thin on top, longish over the ears and neck*]

Boucicault	[*Stepping forward, adjusting his cuffs*] My felicitations to the infernal ringmaster [*Bowing ironically to* PATTERSON]
Patterson	Glory be, for Boosy is himself again.
Boucicault	Call me Dion.
Patterson	Call me Paddy the Clown.

[*The* UNSEEN FIDDLER *now makes an appearance, drifting across the back of the stage, a stooped, homeless figure, shrouded in a shabby, outsize ulster. White hair hangs down from under the wide brim of his battered, dark-green hat; his face is hidden from us*]

Patterson	Jumping Jaysus, who's the Phantom Fiddler?
Boucicault	Father?

Patterson   Father . . . methinks he sees his da!

Boucicault   [*To the* FIDDLER] Look at me. Speak to me!

Patterson   If that's oul' man Boursiquot, he never even was your da, let's
                   face it.

Boucicault   [*Still addressing the* FIDDLER] I have earned your blessing long
                   since, you can no longer deny it!

Patterson   And for why would he want to bless his wife's bastard, pray?

Boucicault   That's a dirty slander, I am this man's son!

Patterson   'Course he never should have married a hot little hussy
                   half his age, that's asking for it, but lo! . . . the guilty party
                   approaches! The upstairs lodger – the Reverend Dr. Dionysius
                   Lardner, a fine fellow-me-lad of Trinity College Dublin . . . and
                   the mammy herself along with him.

                   [*The* PHANTOM FIDDLER, *upstage left, stops playing and stands
                   with head bowed as* ANNE BOURSIQUOT *and* DIONYSIUS LARDNER *enter
                   from the right. (We recognise them at once, since they are the two
                   students whom we saw in the opening scene –* JESSIE MCDERMOT *and*
                   THOMAS BELNAP – *simply adopting these two new roles. They and the
                   other students from scene one will take on all the subsequent roles
                   in similar fashion)*]

                   [ANNE BOURSIQUOT *is in her twenties, flighty and vivacious in a low-
                   cut dress.* LARDNER *is skinny and bespectacled, and has a piping
                   voice*]

                   [*As they enter, he grabs her from behind, nuzzles her neck, and
                   creeps his fingers lewdly into her decolletage. She nestles back
                   against him, her eyes on her husband*]

Boucicault   [*To the* FIDDLER] Show your face to him!

Patterson   Oh, yer man is the Protestant goat all right . . .

Boucicault   STRIKE HIM DOWN!

                   [*But the* PHANTOM FIDDLER *stays where he is, bent and still; and*
                   BOUCICAULT *falls to his knees, burying his head in his arms*]

Anne   [*Pushing* LARDNER *away*] It is no longer in doubt, Dr. Lardner.
                   I am carrying your child. I demand to know your intentions
                   towards it.

Lardner   [*Gesturing at the* FIDDLER] Would the daft oul' codger
                   acknowledge the brat as his own, d'ye supose?

Anne   He will know all too well that it cannot conceivably be his.

Lardner   Not conceivably, no indeed [*With a little snigger*]

Anne   The Boursiquots are, however, a respectable family. Samuel will of course treat the child as his own in the names of propriety and decorum.

Lardner   Grand and glorious names, the pair of them.

                [*And he entwines her in a lascivious embrace*]

Boucicault Cockatrice, usurper! Goatsucker!

Patterson   D'ye mind?

Boucicault Crock-full of cant and cuckoldry!

Patterson   Some of us are trying to watch this, you know. [*To* ANNE BOURSIQUOT, *who has just broken free of the embrace*] Carry on, love.

Anne   [*To* LARDNER] Is it your desire to continue lodging in my house?

Lardner   The accommodation is agreeably commodious, Mrs Boursiquot.

Anne   I shall require two undertakings. One, that you act as guardian to the child with respect to schooling and career. Two, if it prove a boy child, his given names shall be . . . Dionysius Lardner.

Lardner   Is that entirely advisable?

Anne   It is my desire, Dr. Lardner.

Lardner   Then it certainly must and shall be fully satisfied.

Anne   [*Opening her arms to him*] Dionysius!

Lardner   [*Grabbing her*] Mrs Boursiquot!

Patterson   The Age of Steam — and no mistake.

                [*The* PHANTOM FIDDLER *strikes up an anguished cadenza on the violin, and then exits left as* LARDNER *sweeps* ANNE BOURSIQUOT *off on the right*]

Boucicault It's none of it true!

Patterson   You know, if this Lardner fella had only been your uncle . . . you could maybe have played Hamlet instead of the clown. D'ye get it? Ach, get up out of that and quit the catterwailing, it was you that ordered a recount.

Anne	[*From offstage*] Dion!
Patterson	You hear that? Smarten up and act your age, the mammy wants a word with her little lad.
	[BOUCICAULT, *still on his knees, straightens up and dries his eyes like a small boy*]
	[ANNE BOURSIQUOT *enters, goes to him*]
Anne	Dion pet, what are you doing out here, have you been crying, there now, mammy's here . . . [*She cuddles him, kisses his head – he hugs her, still on his knees*] Guess what, pet – Dr. Lardner has a birthday present for you. Look.
	[LARDNER *appears, wreathed in steam from a model traction engine which he is carrying. He sets it down so that it puffs its way towards* BOUCICAULT]
Lardner	Steam, my boy – Steam! The greatest power on God's earth, and it's mine and yours to exploit. [*He picks the model up again*] What do you have to say to that?
Anne	Dr. Lardner is an authority on Steam. Dr. Lardner has written an encyclopedia. In one hundred and thirty-four whole volumes! Just imagine.
Lardner	Tell me, Dion, how would you like to be filthy rich and a power in the land, eh? Whenever you're a big boy?
Anne	Dr. Lardner is going to apprentice you as a civil engineer!
Lardner	You shall assist me to design a railway – all the way from London to Birmingham, my boy. What do you have to say to that?
Boucicault	[*Sullenly*] I want it to come through Dublin.
Lardner	I fear the little man has been missing his geography lessons.
Anne	Indeed he has not, have you pet? He loves school. Tell us what you did in class today, go on, love. What was the lesson today?
Boucicault	Drama.
Anne	Drama? Isn't that grand, Dr. Lardner? Was teacher reading a little play to you's all?
Boucicault	We were acting out a story . . . it was a real good story, it was a man called Oliver Goldsmith, he made it all up, like . . . only teacher wanted us to act out a story of our own after that . . . so I sat down with my jotter . . . and I started to write,

mammy . . . you see, I was making up a story of my own, guardian . . . and I kept on writing and I never stopped, when my ink ran out I switched to pencil, and after a while, before very long, I stopped and looked, and there it was, I wrote a play, I wrote a play, I WROTE A PLAY MOTHER!

[*Music: He leaps to his feet, as they cower before his onslaught*]

Boucicault The magick to conjure spirits, to strike clowns dumb, to amaze princes and emperors, I have it in me, stronger than any steam, you insufferable little swindler . . . .

[LARDNER *turns on his heel and rushes out, and* ANNE *runs after him*]

[*As they vanish*] . . . that's what I learnt in school today, since you ask.

Patterson So much promise in one so young.

Boucicault Telling stuff, though you have to admit. For a schoolboy of sixteen.

Patterson Oh, telling is the word all right.

Anne [*A cry from off*] Dion!

Patterson There's the mammy at it again.

Anne [*Off*] Dion, please, where are you?

Patterson Out here on the stage, missus.

Anne [*Re-entering*] That man has torn the heart from my breast . . . he has taken my life-blood . . .

Boucicault Skedaddled?

Anne My life is over! [*She collapses into her son's arms*]

Boucicault I knew all along he'd abandon you.

Anne He has run away to London, with the wife of Captain Heaviside!

Boucicault [*With dawning delight*] Sweet God above us . . . Heaviside? His partner? He's six-foot-six . . . he's a Guards Captain. He'll break every spidery bone in that cocksure body!

Anne Oh no, don't, I couldn't bear it if he was hurt . . .

Boucicault Him? Hurt That lecherous viper? That steam-inflated huckster?

Anne I will not have any more language, Dion.

Boucicault   That shabby, shoddy little charlatan, that pipsqueak, that wife-plunderer, that shrivelled lump of cold steamed cod-piece, how can you even bear the touch of that smug slimy goat-sucking jumped-up quacksalver of a SCIENTIST, mother, how?

Anne   Oh, God, look at your eyes . . . you're the very spit and image of him!

Boucicault   NOT TRUE!

Anne   I love him and I want him!

[The PHANTOM FIDDLER's tune is heard from off]

Boucicault   Power is all he wants and he's got bored with wielding it in this house . . . listen to me, mother. Lardner is across the water now for good. My father, who is to this Hyperion to a satyr, is here at home in Ireland . . . let pappy back into our house now, give him a chance . . .

Anne   *[Striking him furiously]* You little fool, you know nothing! You have learnt nothing! Boursiquot is a worthless poltroon, a pathetic, puny excuse for a man . . . never speak his name to me again!

[She storms out, as the fiddle music stops abruptly]

Boucicault   *[Calling after her]* Tell me where he lives at least, I need to know him . . . *[Turning to PATTERSON]* Right. I want Lardner back out here immediately.

Patterson   No need to shout. I'm working on it.

Boucicault   I shall play Captain Heaviside myself in this instance.

Patterson   It's only right – sure your acting's always been that way.

Boucicault   Meaning what?

Patterson   On the heavy side.

Boucicault   Music.

[During this exchange, BOUCICAULT has been pulling on a false beard and donning a top hat and opera cloak, from a costume trunk which is part of the stage furniture.

[Piano music begins: The parlour ballad, "O that we two were maying". LARDNER appears, Playing the piano (or miming at an invisible one) with MARY HEAVISIDE standing at his shoulder. They are singing the duet]

O that we two were maying
Down the stream of the soft Spring breeze . . .
Like children with violets playing . . .

[BOUCICAULT *assumes his role as* HEAVISIDE *by thumping at their hotel-room door; the singing abruptly ceases*]

Lardner   Who is it?

Heaviside   Make your peace with God, Lardner.

Mary Heaviside   Merciful heavens, it is Richard!

Lardner   Be quiet, woman, or we are lost.

Mary Heaviside   But what shall we do?

Lardner   Hide yourself. Quickly!

Mary Heaviside   Where, in God's name?

Lardner   Anywhere . . . under the piano.

Heaviside   Don't oblige me to smash the door before I start on you. Lardner.

Lardner   Go on, go on . . . [*Pushing* MARY *under the piano. Calling*] Just one moment.

[*With* MARY HEAVISIDE *crouching under the piano,* LARDNER *opens the door to her husband*]

Lardner   Why, Richard. How agreeable. What brings you to London?

Heaviside   The overnight packet, Dionysius, and then a team of horses . . . helped along by this [*And he produces a horsewhip from under his cloak and cracks it in the air, advancing on* LARDNER]

Lardner   My dear fellow . . . what on earth has got into you?

Heaviside   [*Calling*] Mary! Which hole has this scuttling little cockatrice hidden you in?

Lardner   You must be labouring under some extraordinary misapprehension, Richard . . . aaagh!

[HEAVISIDE *has started whipping him on the buttocks. He races round the piano, pursued by* HEAVISIDE, *who finally catches him and pinions him over the keyboard*]

[MARY *gives a little scream from underneath the piano.* HEAVISIDE *pauses, glances down*]

Heaviside	Ah, there you are, darling, I wondered where you'd got to. Come and join us. [MARY *crawls out, very cowed*] Do forgive my interrupting your music-making. You absolutely must oblige me with a ballad. Try this one. [*Indicating a song in the book on the music stand; and then cracking the whip to get them started*]

[MARY *plays the piano while* LARDNER *rather hoarsely sings*]

[HEAVISIDE *sits a little way off, giving* LARDNER *a taste of the whip at the end of every other line*]

[PATTERSON *meanwhile does a grave litle dance to go with the song*]

Lardner	[*Singing*] Do not trust him, gentle lady,
	Though his voice be low and sweet,
	Heed not him who kneels before thee
	Gently pleading at thy feet.
	Now thy life is in its morning,
	Cloud not this, thy happy lot,
	Listen to the gipsy's warning,
	Gentle lady, trust him not –
	Listen to the gipsy's warning,
	Gentle lady trust him not.

[LARDNER *and* MARY HEAVISIDE *scuttle off, and* BOUCICAULT *discards his* CAPTAIN HEAVISIDE *get-up*]

Boucicault	Such a satisfying scene . . . almost as though I'd written it myself.
Patterson	Ah, I dunno – it wasn't that bad.
Boucicault	It put paid to Lardner at any rate, and may hell roast him now and for evermore amen.
Patterson	Excuse me – but he went on paying your allowance notwithstanding.
Boucicault	My training as an actor was paid for by my mother's cousin, Arthur Guinness.
Patterson	Arthur Guinness? Not actually . . . <u>Arthur Guinness</u>?
Boucicault	He was involved in the brewery trade.
Patterson	We're all quite aware of his trade, thank you. Arthur Guinness . . . sure my wife frequently claimed I was married to the same man.
Boucicault	My mother's side were all wealthy Protestants from the North of Ireland.

Patterson	Oh well, 'nuff said – a thespian type, christened Dionysius, from the wrong side of the blanket, was the one thing they'd always wanted for Christmas, am I right?
Boucicault	Once Guinness discovered the true nature of my vocation, I was disinherited, destitute . . . Dispossessed, as my father had been before me . . .
Patterson	Not the Phantom Fiddler again, in pity's name, will you try at least to move this along a bit. Come on! You tramped the English provinces.

[*The dialogue suddenly accelerates to Fast-Forward*]

Boucicault	I tramped the English provinces, as a jobbing actor, using the name Lee Moreton as a *nom-de-theatre*, until I fetched up in London, in a garret at Charing Cross.
Patterson	The ink froze in your inkwell.
Boucicault	The ink often froze in my inkwell, I was forced to climb into bed fully clothed, and continue writing in pencil . . .
Patterson	There was luckily plenty of lead in your pencil . . .
Boucicault	. . . working away all night underneath the blankets.
Patterson	. . . as many a piece of fluff will bear witness.

[BOUCICAULT *clutches his forehead, sways a little, and the pace returns to normal*]

Boucicault	What are you doing to me? Where am I?
Patterson	You have planted your foot in the heart of the British Empire's stage . . . and said, "This spot is mine"
Boucicault	What is the name of this theatre?
Patterson	What, this? This is London's own famous Covent Garden Theatre, Boosy . . .

[*A free standing theatre stage-door has appeared*]

. . . the cathedral of the legitimate drama in England. You beat a pious pilgrimage to its door often enough, in your Lee Moreton days. [*Knocks on the stage door*] Until one day they finally let you in.

[*The door is whipped open and a hawk-faced stage doorman looks out; the pace hots up again*]

Doorman	Soliciting is prohibited, whether from hawkers, beggars, pedlars, ponces, would-be players or self-styled playwrights, thank you and good morning.

[BOUCICAULT *plants a swift foot in the door before it can be closed*]

Boucicault	Good morning, my card. [*Presenting it*]
Doorman	[*Glancing at it*] Mr Morton. One hour late.
Boucicault	Late for what?
Doorman	Step in please.

[BOUCICAULT *steps through the door, the* DOORMAN *closes it, and presents* BOUCICAULT *with a written note*]

Doorman	From Mr Charles Matthews. Whom I shall now apprise of your entrance.

[*The* DOORMAN *exits.* PATTERSON *darts forward to read the note over* BOUCICAULT's *shoulder*]

Boucicault	[*Reading*] "My dear Maddison" . . . oh, good God.
Patterson	What's going on?
Boucicault	The doorman has misread my card, he thinks I'm Maddison Morton instead of Lee Moreton.
Patterson	Who's this Maddison Morton?
Boucicault	A famous author of farces.
Patterson	Tell us this – are you making it all up as you go along?
Boucicault	I could never presume to compete with my own life for sheer inventiveness.

[CHARLES MATTHEWS *enters. He is in costume as the Hunchback of Notre Dame, and is engrossed in reading a manuscript. He doesn't look up at* BOUCICAULT]

Matthews	Y'know, I have a definite hunch about this play . . . the hiding under the piano, Maddison. It's a bit improbable, even for a farce, don't you think so?
Boucicault	Mr Matthews . . .
Matthews	Mmm? [*Glancing up; double-take*] Great heavens – you're not Maddison Morton. You're not even a grown man.
Belnap	Mistaken identity, at the door, sir, tried to explain got rushed on in, most embarrassing . . . off I go . . .
Matthews	What brought you here in the first place?

Boucicault	Fact is, sir — I submitted a little piece of my own some months back, under the name of Lee Moreton.
Matthews	I see, I see, look here my boy, we are inundated with plays, I fear, far more than we can ever read, I shall have my secretary return your script. How is it entitled?
Matthews	*A Lover By Proxy*, sir.
Matthews	I beg your pardon?
Boucicault	*A Lover By Proxy.*

[MATTHEWS, *astonished, examines the title page of the script in his hand*]

Matthews	How supremely droll . . . look here, Mr Moreton, it is the very play I have been reading! Yes, look, "by L. Moreton Esquire", I assumed it was Maddison's, I have misread your name just as my doorman did!
Patterson	This is so ridiculous, I'm nearly inclined to believe it.
Boucicault	Might I dare hope for a production, sir?
Matthews	A production? [*Richly amused*] Oh lord no, dear boy, there's no possibility of that. The British public no longer believes in farces.
Boucicault	What do they believe in now, Mr. Matthews?
Matthews	Circuses.
Patterson	Surprising how sensible the British can sometimes be.

[MATTHEWS *tosses the script to* BOUCICAULT]

Matthews	Never mind, we're all square now, cheerio! [*And he makes to leave*]
Boucicault	[*In desperation*] Tell me, sir, what kind of play do you most long to read?
Matthews	Oh, a thumping good five-act comedy of modern life, I imagine . . . [*And he is gone*]

[BOUCICAULT *prowls around the stage, as the action returns once again to a walking pace*]

| Boucicault | It was all I needed to hear. Farquhar, Congreve, Sheridan, Goldsmith . . . Comedy of Manners! Wit, elegance, refinement of feeling, a wise and genial exercise for civilised minds, the very art I most humbly aspired to practise! |

Patterson	Comedy be damned, all that high-falutin antiquarian repartee . . .
Boucicault	What in hell would you know, you insignificant pig-ignorant pratfall-merchant!
Patterson	Such wit and elegance, such refinement of feeling . . . and furthermore you never did nothing humbly from the day and hour your mother relieved herself of you.

[*He has knocked on the stage door again, and the* DOORMAN *opens it before* BOUCICAULT *can get a reply in. The action accelerates once more*]

Doorman	Tinkers, tailors and tarts need not apply, likewise aspiring actors and dramatists, foundlings, and the mothers of foundlings, thank you and good afternoon.

[BOUCICAULT *thrusts an even speedier foot in the door*]

Boucicault	Good afternoon, my card. [*Giving it to him*]
Doorman	[*Glancing at it*] Mr Boucicault. Never heard of you.
Boucicault	Pray tell Mr. Charles Matthews I have something to give him.

[MATTHEWS *has wandered on, once again in his hunchback costume*]

Matthews	[*To the* DOORMAN] Is that the postboy?
Boucicault	[*Calling*] Me again, sir, saw you four weeks ago, said you wanted a five-act comedy of modern manners, am now in a position to supply same.
Matthews	The Irish boy, is that it?
Boucicault	May I come in?
Matthews	Morton, wasn't it?

[MATTHEWS *has come as far as the door, so that* BOUCICAULT *is able to reach past the doorman and thrust his script into* MATTHEWS' *hands*]

Boucicault	For you, sir.
Matthews	Good lord, whatever is this . . . [*Reading*] "Out of Town, A Comedy in Five Acts" . . . do you mean to say you have composed this since I saw you the other day?
Boucicault	Such as it is, sir.
Matthews	Most remarkable.
Patterson	Entirely nauseating.

Boucicault   Might you have the time to consider it, sir?

Matthews   Well . . . why not? My wife Madame Vestris and I are reading scripts over the weekend, we shall try your little effort out on our house guests, Mr Morton.

Boucicault   Actually, sir, it's Boucicault – Dion Boucicault.

Matthews   Aha, you have adopted a fancy stage name, isn't it rather a mouthful, though? never mind, dear boy, it certainly sounds more theatrical than Charles Matthews, what?

[He exits laughing and the DOORMAN *promptly shuts the door in* BOUCICAULT*'s face]*

[The action slows down again]

*[*BOUCICAULT *stalks around the stage grim-faced]*

Boucicault   He sprawls out on his ottoman in front of a glowing hearth, snorting into a large cognac, madame resplendent in her latest gown, the distinguished guests disposed about the warmly-lit room . . . and outside, in the dark empty yawn of an indifferent world, you prowl the streets, incapable of rest, dispossessed and starving. You pass and pass and press your face against the window, devouring the picture of them in there, plump with wit and wine, their flesh creamy with pleasure as they breathe in the intoxication of their own fame and power . . . power over you and all your kind! You stare in till your eyes are burnt hollow, watching them idly at play upon your name, upon your parentage, at play upon your provincialism, at play upon your PLAY! and all the while the monstrous ache, the lust you feel, to be let in, to burst the muzzle and gorge down the entire room, by Christ I would cheerfully kill the goatsucker, and eat the floral tributes off his hearse SINGLE-HANDED!

Patterson   A wise and genial exercise for civilised minds . . .

[And PATTERSON *knocks on the stage door, which is whipped open as before by the* DOORMAN*]*

[The pace accelerates]

Doorman   Stage-door Johnnies, Champagne Charlies, Hooray Henrys and Jack-the-Lads not admitted, thank you and good evening, oh, it's you, sir.

Boucicault   By appointment.

Doorman   Step in, please, I shall apprise Mr Matthews of your entrance.

Boucicault   Do so. [*As he steps through the door*]

Doorman   But soft – he approaches.

[*The* DOORMAN *unctuously departs as* MATTHEWS *appears, still the hunchback and still clutching the script*]

Matthews   Boucicault, my dear boy, permit me to dissipate your anxiety on the instant – Madame and I are enchanted with your piece, so much so that we have resolved to put it into production forthwith, you must come and read it to the company next Friday. There will of course be alterations necessary, but you must excuse me or I shall miss my entrance!

[*He thrusts the script into* BOUCICAULT*'s hands and rushes off. And the bells of Notre Dame peal out in joyful din*]

[BOUCICAULT *raises his arms to heaven in thanksgiving, throws himself down, drums his heels on the floor, rolls around laughing hysterically – then leaps to his feet. The bells abruptly stop*]

Boucicault   What alterations?

Patterson   Ah, jaysus – I've got that terrible yawn you get in the large intestine, when somebody says, this is where the story really begins.

[*The backdrop parts, to reveal* CHARLES MATTHEWS, MADAME VESTRIS *and the members of their company standing in a line and applauding. They have been listening to* BOUCICAULT *reading aloud his play. He moves up towards them, having reached the final speech.*]

Boucicault   [*Reading*] "Max Harkaway":– "Permit me to correct you on one point. Bare-faced assurance is the vulgar substitute for gentlemanly ease; and there are many who, by aping the vices of the great, imagine that they elevate themselves to the ranks of those whose faults alone they copy. No, sir! The title of gentleman is the only one out of any monarch's gift, yet within the reach of every peasant. It should be engrossed by Truth – stamped with Honour – sealed with good-feeling – signed Man – and enrolled in every true young English heart."

[*The Company, wreathed in smiles of approval, applauds with gusto*]

Madame Vestris   Bravo, indeed, and now off to the greenroom with us all, to toast our brilliant young scribe with a glass of champagne. Lead the way, Mrs Nisbet.

[*They all stroll off chatting excitedly, except for* MATTHEWS, *who draws* BOUCICAULT *aside, and* VESTRIS, *who hangs back also*]

Matthews	Now then, my young lion, how are we to make this piece of yours work on the stage?
Boucicault	Sir?
Matthews	Let us consider my own character, merely as an example – it won't do to have him Irish, you know, won't do at all. It means playing him as a garrulous buffoon . . . let him be droll, let him scintillate! We really mustn't call him Mulvather. Make him English! Let us call him – Dazzle.
Boucicault	Pardon me, sir . . . but that is already the name of Mr Farren's character. Sir William Dazzle.
Matthews	Quite so, dear boy – you must find a new name for Billy's part also, but not to worry, there's time enough for that.
Madame Vestris	[*Intervening*] Dion, my darling, this title, *Out of Town* – it's much too homespun for such a momentous debut, it makes the wrong emphasis, the title should rather proclaim your arrival in our midst, your triumph over wild and primitive origins, it should hoist your banner, you are assured of a great success in the premier theatre in England – what do you say to *London Assurance*?
Boucicault	[*To* PATTERSON] Get them off.
Patterson	Are you talking to her or to me?
Matthews	How clever, darling. Absolutely! *London Assurance*!
Boucicault	Get them off, for God's sake!
Patterson	All right, they're going, they're going.
	[*And the backdrop closes again, shutting* MATTHEWS *and* VESTRIS *out*]
Patterson	The fact remains – she certainly got your number very nicely with that title.
Boucicault	It was still my own work at the end of all!
Patterson	Did I say it wasn't? Even if you did walk out on the opening night?
Boucicault	I was a boy of twenty. I couldn't bear it out there, in the lap of the beast, I fled away into the dark . . . I found myself on Waterloo Bridge, in the rain, my cheek was pressed against a wet stone balustrade, to try and quench the fire in it . . .
Patterson	You had caught a germ in the blood, Boosy, that sudden terrible doubt – maybe I'm not the genius I thought I was up till eight o'clock this evening. Farquhar, Sheridan, Goldsmith – Irishmen all, but conquerors of the English stage – and taking

over the torch now, Dionysius Lardner Boucicault! Quote –
"Mr Boucicault's *London Assurance* is the legitimate heir of
*The Recruiting Officer, She Stoops to Conquer, The School for
Scandal* . . . in brief, he is the authentic comedy genius of the
Age" . . . that was what you were petrified they wouldn't say,
am I right?

Boucicault	I walked back to the theatre, it was ringing with laughter and cheers, I rushed in, the place was jammed, I saw the final scene, there was a cataclysm of joy, I was manhandled on to the stage to receive the roar of the beast, the curtain descended for the final time, I was engulfed in rapture!
Patterson	Yeah, I know the feeling.
Boucicault	You? You have no idea what I'm talking about, don't try to compare the circus ring with the legitimate stage!
Patterson	Fine word, legitimate.
Boucicault	I was acclaimed as the great rising dramatic poet of the Age!
Patterson	Now, gods, stand up for bastards.

[*The backdrop parts again, to reveal the* London Assurance
*company holding their final bow, and then straightening up from
it.* CHARLES MATTHEWS *steps downstage towards* BOUCICAULT]

Matthews	My dear boy. The gods have indeed smiled upon us. The heavens beckon. Speak your heart to us.
Boucicault	I am struck dumb.
Matthews	[*Taking him by the hand*] Come.

[*He leads* BOUCICAULT *up to* MADAME VESTRIS *and* MRS NISBET]

Matthews	There. Does not the company of angels inspire you to eloquence? What do you have to say to your leading ladies?

[BOUCICAULT *puts his arms round the two women's waists*]

Boucicault	[*Ravenously*] KISS ME!

[VESTRIS *offers up her mouth, and he falls upon it, then upon*
NISBET'*s*]

[*The band strikes up a triumphant intro. to* "The Garden Where the
Praties Grow" – *then continues on to the first line, which* PATTERSON
sings]

Patterson	Have you ever been in love, my boys, Or did you feel the pain . . .

[The band stops]

*[*BOUCICAULT *has finished kissing* MRS NISBET *and is shaking hands with the other members of the company as they drift off. He is finally left with* MATTHEWS, *who draws him into a private colloquy. All this is happening upstage as* PATTERSON *continues with his patter and singing]*

Patterson   I had a pal once worked in a freak show. The Living Skeleton – that was his billing. He was a vegetarian drinker – he would drink anything out of a bottle so long as it wasn't milk or beef tea. But the best of it is – his name was Coffin! I kid you not. Mickey Coffin.

[The band resumes, he sings]

I'd rather be in gaol myself
Than be in love again . . .

[The band stops, he speaks]

Mickey the Living Skeleton and me came from the County Clare. Born in the same village, the same year, 1840. Growing up with the same stench. Sweet sickly breath on the land. By the time we were nine all the other boys were dead of hunger – potato blight they called it – so Mickey went out on the road as a Living Skeleton, and as for me – I wrote this song.

[The band resumes, he sings]

Though the girl I loved was beautiful,
I'd have you all to know
That I met her in the garden where the praties grow!

[End music]

*[*MATTHEWS *has now followed the company off.* BOUCICAULT *re-joins* PATTERSON]*

Boucicault   What do you mean plaguing the stage with all that?

Patterson   Just practising me act. I got tired of watching yours.

Boucicault   My life is the one in the balance! Yours is already consigned to limbo and you're more than welcome to return to it.

Patterson   Will we go, then?

Boucicault   As it happens, I'm only just getting started.

Patterson   "Permit me to correct you on one point:.the title of gentleman is the only one out of any monarch's gift, yet within the reach of every peasant . . . " tell us, Boosy – how many peasants

have you actually met? I'd say that I'm your first and last, and
speaking for Mickey Coffin and me, you can stick your title of
gentleman, we'd sooner be seen dead, thanks.

Boucicault   You're a peasant snob, Patterson. You think to be poor and to
suffer is a superior state of being, mouldering away in some
boghole in Connacht, but there is no shred of virtue in being a
victim – history disables all of us, in whatever fashion, it's the
use to which we put our disabilities, that's virtue – not how
much we suffer them – it's how we act upon them!

Patterson   So tell us, Mr Boucicault, how did you react during the Great
Irish Famine? – Oh, I kept London well supplied with me
comedies of manners.

Boucicault   As opposed to being a clown in a travelling circus, let's say?

Patterson   I kept faith with my own people, as a true clown should.

Boucicault   And I kept faith with my own work, as a true artist must, to
make a living thing that endures . . .

Anne   [*Calling from off*] Dion!

Patterson   There's the mammy arrived from Dublin.

Boucicault   [*Still to* PATTERSON] . . . a thing that endures – that is the sole
redress we have, against history and all its crimes.

Patterson   You can speechify, Boosy – but you've been a clown all along
and a false one at that.

[ANNE BOURSIQUOT *enters, in coat and hat*]

Anne   Dion dearest!

Boucicault   [*Going to her*] Mother!

Anne   [*Embracing*] Oh, my little lad, you have worked such wonders!
But you needn't have sent us so much money.

Boucicault   I have a house in Pembroke Square, mother. I have a carriage
and two horses, I wanted you here to see it all for yourself.

Anne   I'm so relieved you've given up the acting, pet, it had my
entire connection scandalised.

Boucicault   Listen to me, mother. This is only the start. A New Age is on
the rise, and my star along with it, it's the birth of opportunity
for anybody with the determination to seize it, irrespective of
who you are or where you come from. I have planted my foot
in the heart of the Empire's stage, and said – This spot is mine!

Anne	You're the mirror image of Dionysius, every word you utter could be his!
Boucicault	Don't mention that little goatsucker's name.
Anne	I hope you've written and told him your good fortune.
Boucicault	I want my father's address, I want him to know, I want him to see my play, where is he?
Anne	You know very well that Boursiquot has been dead to me for fourteen years past!
Boucicault	He may be buried somewhere in Ireland, but he is not yet quite dead, just tell me where he works.
Anne	Go home and find him for yourself, if it means so much to you!
	[*She turns on her heel*]
Boucicault	Mother! [*She pauses*] On Monday night my new play opens. *The Irish Heiress.* I have arranged for you and William to have the best seats in the house.
Anne	Your brother is arranging accommodation, I must join him.
	[*She walks on out*]
Boucicault	But you'll be staying at Pembroke Square . . .
	[PATTERSON *has produced a newspaper with an ostentatious flourish. He reads aloud from it*]
Patterson	"It was interesting to observe whether the author had progressed . . . whether he had elevated himself to something like a position as a producer of dramatic literature . . . *The Irish Heiress* is not an advance. It is as much a farce as *London Assurance*, and it is a weak farce instead of a strong one. There is the same want of creative power, but there is not the same buoyance and spirit; there is the similar selection of well-tried means, but the same taste is no longer employed, and the result is feeble and inefficient."
Boucicault	Are THEY down there?
Patterson	To whom do you refer?
Boucicault	Them – those wens and warts, those goitres on the throat of poetry, those styes in the eye of inspiration, those tapeworms of a theatrical culture . . .
Patterson	The actors?

Boucicault   The critics!

Patterson   Oh, the critics, oh yeah – the critics are all down below all
                      right, you can certainly count on that.

Boucicault   In which case do your damnedest, but you will never contain
                      me in any hell I have to share with them. They crucified me!

Patterson   Excuse me, but that would have put you in a different league
                      altogether.

Boucicault   Every play I offered was violated by them, mocked, debased,
                      trampled into the dirt.

Patterson   They were only doing their job, sure the public had no
                      stomach for all that fustian backchat.

Boucicault   Oh yes, the roar of the beast, that too . . . I was writing comedy
                      of manners for a people who has passed beyond manners,
                      beyond comedy. A New Age on the rise, oh yes . . . plunder
                      and pig-ignorance, a New Dark Age of blood force, the likes of
                      Lardner with his scientific baubles, millions enslaved by them,
                      a raw-boned British master-race, clothing their barbarism
                      in piety and pinstripes and fairy-princess sugar candy, what
                      entertainment does such an age demand, do you suppose?

Benjamin Webster
                      [*Suddenly entering*] Melodrama, Dion. The people want
                      melodrama.

                      [WEBSTER *is a theatre manager, raw-boned, British and dressed in
                      pinstripes*]

Boucicault   Enter Benjamin Webster.

Patterson   So which theatre is this?

Boucicault   The Haymarket in London. He's the proprietor.

Patterson   [*To* WEBSTER] How'd y'do?

Webster   [*Oblivious to this*] The French, Dion, look at the French.
                      Boulevards ahead of us, in the melodrama stakes. Why not pop
                      over to Paris and see what you can gather up?

                      [BOUCICAULT *has sat down with a mirror and a make-up box, at the
                      moment of* WEBSTER'*s entrance, and has begun to transform himself
                      into* ALAN RABY, *the title role in his play* The Vampire. *He continues
                      with this throughout the scene that follows, with* PATTERSON *acting
                      as his dresser*]

Boucicault	Listen, Webster. I laboured for six months over *Old Heads and Young Hearts*, you can afford to pay me more than one hundred pounds for it, damn you!
Webster	Market forces, Dion. Personally I subscribe to the Free Trade League, I mean look at it with common sense. I can pop over to Paris, see how a play is taking the stage, invest twenty-five pounds in a translation, and presto – I have a hit. Whereas some unknown quantity of yours is going to mean risking hundreds. I mean, *Old Heads and Young Hearts* is a sound enough comedy in its way . . .
Boucicault	Charles Matthews and Madame Vestris will get three thousand a year for appearing in it!
	[CHARLES MATTHEWS *enters*]
Matthews	It will not run for a week, dear boy, let alone a year.
	[MADAME VESTRIS *follows him on*]
Boucicault	Certainly not the way you're playing it, Matthews. Having engineered your own bankruptcy, you now appear determined to achieve mine.
Matthews	My dear boy, with your brute appetite for houses, clothes and carriages, along with gaming, wining, dining, whoring and borrowing, you are entirely self-sufficient in that regard.
Madame Vestris	Our author has a young head. With a very old heart.
Boucicault	[*To* WEBSTER] They are perfectly entitled to write a play, but they are not entitled to write my play!
Madame Vestris	We took your wild scribblings and fashioned them into a play called *London Assurance*, that is our business, though you have soon enough forgotten it.
Boucicault	Your business is to utter what I create, I want no-one's opinions but my own as to the consistency of my characters.
Matthews	Very well, you shall have none but your own. As from now, you no longer have a company.
	[MATTHEWS *and* VESTRIS *stride off*]
Webster	I shall of course persuade them to stay on, at a price. As for you, Dion – it's back home to the bog, I'm afraid.
Boucicault	They would never have treated Oliver Goldsmith like a hired clerk!
Webster	Tell me something – did you study French at school as well as Oliver Goldsmith?

Boucicault   My French is impeccable.

[*He has now finished making himself up as the vampire, with "livid face and fixed look"* (Queen Victoria). PATTERSON *helps him into the* ALAN RABY *Cloak and tunic – with the chained bible hanging from the belt – during the next speech*]

Webster   Here then is my offer. Set up shop in Paris. For every play you purloin and re-fashion, I shall pay you fifty pounds. I have even taken the trouble to draw up a contract [*Producing it from his inside pocket*] You should clear three thousand a year quite comfortably.

Boucicault   So. You have gone so far as to calculate my price.

Webster   Merely the price of the style in which you are now accustomed to live. There is of course the artistic option, ink frozen in the inkwell, obscure and bitter penury, all that kind of thing.

Boucicault   [*Taking the contract*] Very well, Webster. I shall sell myself into perdition. Watch out for the free market, though. One day it may be me who is buying you. [*And he signs the contract on* PATTERSON's *bent back*]

Webster   Oh, absolutely, Dion.

[BOUCICAULT *hands over the signed contract to* WEBSTER, *who pockets it and departs*]

Webster   [*As he goes*] Much obliged.

Patterson   [*Shouting into the wings*] Right you are, he's sold himself! To the highest bidder! You can give him the girl now, go ahead, send her on!

[*Vampire wedding music*]

[*Snow covered mountains appear*]

[*Enter* ANNE GUIOT – *from* BOUCICAULT's The Vampire *in a filmy wedding dress and veil*]

[BOUCICAULT *has become* ALAN RABY]

Raby   At last. She is here. Tonight, ere the moon rises, a new life drawn from the pure heart of a maiden must enter into this form. Her life for mine!

Anne   [*French accent*] What do I hear?

Raby   You hear that I love you. Anne, my soul, are you not mine?

Anne   What power is this that oppresses me?

Raby   It is my will; mine eyes fix upon thy heart as if with fangs, while my soul like a serpent entwines thine within its folds, and crushes thee to my will. Anne, thou art mine!

Anne   Spare me. Yes, thou art my master; I cannot oppose thee.

Raby   [*Taking her by the hand*] You are robed for the altar . . . I will take you there.

[*He begins leading her up the mountainside*]

Raby   My will beckons thee to come.

Anne   I obey. I obey . . .

Raby   She is mine!

[*As they reach the mountain peak, the macabre wedding music wells up.* RABY *lifts back* ANNE's *veil and bends down as though to kiss her – but instead sinks his teeth into her neck*]

[*She gives a deathly cry and falls off the mountain out of sight.* RABY *turns his bloodstained mouth and outstretched arms in triumph towards the new moon rising. Then, as the music peaks, he sweeps back down*]

[*The lights change, the music finishes, and* BOUCICAULT *is once more standing in front of his make-up box, and of a mirror held by* PATTERSON, *wiping the blood off his mouth*]

Patterson   So. Are you going to tell us or not?

Boucicault   Tell you what?

Patterson   Did she fall off that mountain or did you push her?

Boucicault   Neither.

Patterson   You're not pretending you were never married to a French heiress?

Boucicault   For a time I was. A brief time.

Patterson   So how did she die?

Boucicault   Like most people. By degrees.

Patterson   You mean there was nothing perpendicular to it?

Boucicault   That rumour was a journalistic fiction from start to finish.

Patterson   Although she didn't exactly leave you hard up.

Boucicault   She belonged to the nobility.

Patterson	Nice going, Boosy. She was your very first adaptation from the French – am I right? Tell you one thing – she was a lot easier to credit than some of them other melodramas you brought back with you.
Boucicault	All I did was honour the bond, to supply the beast with all its orders . . . lust, greed and sadism framed around with hearts and flowers . . . a faithful mirror of the Empire.
Patterson	You loved it!
Boucicault	Melodrama was the raw fuel of the Age, nothing less – crude and explosive like the base culture it energised, it is literally child's play, if you've ever bothered to observe children play-acting, I was obliged to cater to child-like minds! Charles Kean's amongst them.
Patterson	Ah holy God, spare us another flint-hearted theatre manager.
Boucicault	He had the biggest hits in his career from me, it was of no account, I was still the pariah, beyond the pale, unworthy.
Patterson	For what?
Boucicault	For Agnes Robertson, what else . . . his darling ward and protege, the most breathtaking girl of nineteen I had ever laid eyes on.
Patterson	And you've laid eyes on a few.
Boucicault	I played the Vampire to her sweet English virgin . . . my own play, my own production, we took Kean's theatre by storm!
	[*The Vampire music again.* PATTERSON *flees into the wings.* BOUCICAULT *turns back into* ALAN RABY]
Raby	Now for my new bride. Agnes! Agnes, arise! – she obeys me. Come, I command thee! – so, she approaches – she is a slave to my will!
	[*Enter* AGNES ROBERTSON, *in a trance and a flimsy night-dress*]
Agnes	I am here.
Raby	[*Making to embrace her*] Agnes . . .
Agnes	Touch me not, thy touch strikes cold into my heart – oh, let me sleep.
Raby	Why do you look thus upon me?
Agnes	Begone! You inspire me with terror.

Raby	Thou lovest me, thy soul is mine, come to my heart, thou can'st not escape the spell my spirit has cast upon thine. Why do you repulse . . .
Agnes	Because that breast upon which you press me, seems to be the bosom of a corpse, and from the heart within I feel no throb of life!
Raby	Ah! Dost thou know me, then?
Agnes	Away – Phantom! Demon! – thy soul is dark, thy heart is cold.
Raby	Agnes – thy life must pass into that heart.
Agnes	Avaunt! – leave me! – my father . . . my guardian . . . oh, my voice is choked with fear . . . avoid thee, fiend! abhorrent spectre..!

[*He kisses her; she returns the kiss*]

Raby	She is mine!

[*And he buries his face in her neck, as she clutches him in a passionate embrace*]

[*As the music ends and the lights change, they disengage from the embrace, with* BOUCICAULT *now playing himself again*]

Boucicault	My fiery little star . . . It is not yet too late to change course, you know.
Agnes	You may change, Dion. I know now I never will.
Boucicault	Your guardian believes there is no room for my like in civilised society.
Agnes	It's only because you're a vampire.
Boucicault	He informed me that you were his ward, that you were betrothed to the Earl of Hopetoun, and that my employment with him was hereby terminated.
Agnes	What did you say?
Boucicault	I said, actually Mr Kean, it goes like this – the Earl of Hopetoun is a joke. You are an old woman. Agnes is affianced to me. We both hereby resign.
Agnes	He'll do all in his power to separate us.
Boucicault	New York is beyond his power, Agnes, and the power of all his kind . . . a mansion of the dispossessed, for generations of my own people, a place of transfiguration, I'm going to forge myself a new soul in a new world, and you along with me!

Agnes   Dion, surely it could be arranged for us to travel out together . . .

Boucicault   I've already told you. There are certain affairs that I have to settle, before I go.

Agnes   What affairs?

Boucicault   My father's.

[*The* PHANTOM FIDDLER'*s music is heard*]

Agnes   I can wait for that . . .

Boucicault   However – the work in New York will not wait for you, you have to go there at once, Agnes.

Agnes   I should like to meet your father.

Boucicault   So would I, but I don't think you'd like the look of him.

Agnes   How can you say that . . .

Boucicault   He's been dead since April.

Agnes   My poor Dion . . . how so?

Boucicault   It appears he had been working in a brewery all these years . . . in the town of Athlone, it's dead in the centre of Ireland, furthest away you can get from any coast, more or less. I expect he felt safe there. I wanted his blessing on my work . . . I seem to have frightened him. Do I frighten you?

Agnes   I do sometimes wonder if you really are a vampire.

Boucicault   Of course I'm not, not during daylight hours.

Agnes   You never see daylight, the way you live.

Boucicault   I shall be seeing a lot more of it than I care for, between Liverpool and New York.

Agnes   So shall I, Dion – between New York and you.

[*She kisses him lightly and exits. He looks after her, lost in thought*]

[*The* PHANTOM FIDDLER *appears upstage, as before, playing away.* BOUCICAULT *sees him, moves up towards him*]

Boucicault   Father . . . have you no word to say to me?

[*The* FIDDLER *suddenly swings around. He has a death's head.* BOUCICAULT *cries out in fear and falls down in a dead faint*]

Phantom Fiddler   This is my beloved son, in whom I am well pleased – HEAR YE HIM!

[*And with a bloodcurdling laugh, he whips off the hat and skull mask to reveal himself as* JOHNNY PATTERSON]

[*The band strikes up with "The Garden where the Praties Grow"*]

Patterson   [*Singing*] Have you ever been in love, my boys,
Or did you feel the pain,
I'd rather be in gaol myself
Than be in love again,
Though the girl I loved was beautiful
I'd have you all to know
That I met her in the garden where the praties grow!

[*The band stops. But the* PHANTOM FIDDLER's *lament continues faintly throughout the following speech*]

Patterson   Funny you should mention Liverpool, Boosy — it was the first place I ever sang that song. I'd only just finished writing it, on the road, with Pablo Fanqué's circus.

[*Sings unaccompanied*] She was singing an old Irish song,
Called "Gradh Geal mo croid-he" . . .

[*Speaks*] It was an entirely Irish audience in Liverpool, that night, most of them still speaking the ould tongue. They'd come over twenty years previous. Driven out. Refugees from the Famine.

[*Sings unaccompanied*] Oh boys, says I, what a wife she'd make
For an Irish lad like me . . .

[*Speaks*] I was orphaned very young, I grew up with the smell. My uncle enlisted me, I was a drummer boy, I marched with the regiment, along by the ditches piled high with misshapen corpses, with the mouths stained green from eating grass and docken.

[*Sings unaccompanied*] I was on important business but I did not like to go,
And leave the girl and garden where the praties grow . . .

[*Speaks*] The praties. The taties, the spuds . . . the potatoes. That was what failed, Boosy, every garden a family grave, sick-sweet and stinking. Little children like stick effigies. Mumbling on the shrivelled dugs of mothers scarcely adult, already senile. Famine . . . not a man, woman or youngster in that audience whose destiny wasn't ordained by it, who hadn't lost a mother, father, brother, sister, husband, wife, sweetheart, country, why? Why? WHY?

[*The fiddle music abruptly stops*]

Patterson   [*Sings rapidly, still unaccompanied*]
She was just the sort of creature, boys,
That nature did intend
To walk straight through the world, my boys,
Without a Grecian bend,
Nor did she wear a chignon, I'll have you all to know
That I met her in the garden where the praties grow . . .

[*Speaks*] I sang on to the end , and I heard neither laughter nor
jeers, but a long low moan – the keen of grief for the phantom
generations with us there in the tent – and I felt the humility
and privilege of my clown's motley, and was proud.

[*The band strikes up the tune again*]

Patterson   [*Full performance*]
Says I, my pretty fair maid, I hope you'll pardon me,
But she wasn't like those city girls that would say, "you're
making free",
She answered me right modestly and curtsied very low,
Saying, "you're welcome to the garden where the praties
grow" –
She was just the sort of creature, boys,
That nature did intend
To walk straight through the world, my boys,
Without a Grecian bend –
Nor did she wear a chignon, I'll have you all to know
That I met her in the garden where the praties grow!

[*The band stops*]

[PATTERSON *goes over to where* BOUCICAULT *is lying. and hooks him
under his armpits in order to hoist him to his feet*]

Patterson   So you see, Boosy, we've had enough of vampires, the
country's life blood sucked dry . . . time to turn in now, come
on, let's shift!

[*The band strikes up a demented version of the fiddle air.* PATTERSON,
holding BOUCICAULT *under the arms from behind, dances him
round the stage and on to the trap, which begins to descend, with*
PATTERSON *roaring with laughter as* BOUCICAULT *struggles helplessly
in his arms*]

[*Lights fade to black*]

[*End of Act 1*]

Act 2

[*From below the stage,* BOUCICAULT *and* PATTERSON *ascend once more on the trap*]

[BOUCICAULT *is middle-aged now, bald on top, morose. He is on his knees.* PATTERSON *is brushing him down*]

Patterson   There you go, Boosy. There's no harm done. [*Raising him to his feet*] That's you to rights. You're as right as rain again.

Boucicault   I do not consider rain to be the epitome of rightness.

Patterson   Touché, very rich! – and you thinking you were a goner there, just for a bit.

Boucicault   It appears you are entertained by playing the fool with me.

Patterson   Sure playing the fool is the one talent we have, you and me both . . . naw, it was just a little false alarm to gee you up a bit, I mean, no harm intended but I do have a matinee today.

Boucicault   What do you mean? You can't still perform?

Patterson   Divil the bit else, it's part of the deal. All your celebrated performances, Boosy – you'll be repeating them all, ad infinitum, only difference being, there's no exits anymore . . . and no audience, of course. That's the meaning of limbo in the show business. On for the duration, all by yourself, no earthly stars and no heavenly bodies . . . just this. Are you ready for it yet?

[BOUCICAULT *moves away from the trap*]

Boucicault   I can smell blood.

Patterson   Where can we be?

Boucicault   New York City, where else.

Patterson   Your favourite theatre!

Boucicault   Far more than just a theatre – a non-stop street carnival, a world's fair, a bazaar of the nations, an adolescent girl's heart with the head of a brutal businessman!

Patterson   Did you write that or was it for real?

Boucicault   Wall Street. [*Produces a notebook, consults it*] The crash of 1837. A crooked banker is on the point of defaulting on his debts. His name – is Gideon Bloodgood.

[AGNES *enters, pushing a baby carriage*]

Agnes   I thought I would show little Eve her very first theatre.

[BOUCICAULT *is trying out the role of* BLOODGOOD]

Boucicault   So, as I expected, every stock is down further still, and my last effort to retrieve my fortune has plunged me into utter ruin . . .

Agnes   Dion!

Boucicault   But all is prepared for my flight with my only care in life, my only hope, my darling child, her fortune is secure . . .

Agnes   Oh, it's something you're writing! For a moment I took you seriously.

Boucicault   That's not like you, Agnes. [*Looking into the baby carriage*] Well, little Eve — it's no garden of Eden here, is it? Look at her, she's a perfect image of you. A proper Fairy Star.

Agnes   I hate them calling me that.

Boucicault   Are you feeling any stronger today, Agnes?

Agnes   Strong enough to come this far . . . what do you mean?

Boucicault   Tomorrow New York will ring from Union Square to the Battery with the news — Bloodgood has absconded!

Agnes   You surely can't want me to start again already?

[PATTERSON *suddenly takes over the* BLOODGOOD *role*]

Patterson   Yonder street, now so still, will be filled with a howling multitude, for the house of Bloodgood the banker will fail, and in its fall will crash hundreds, thousands, who have their fortunes laid up here . . .

Agnes   Dion, I can't face the road again, not yet.

Boucicault   But tomorrow I shall be safe on board the packet for Liverpool!

Agnes   We had four continuous years of it, I know what you are going to say, I was on stage again within the month after little Willie's birth, but I have two of them to cope with now . . .

Boucicault   All I asked was, are you feeling stronger? Apparently you are. Where is little Willie, by the way?

Agnes   Zoe took him to the circus.

Patterson   Good on you, Zoe.

Boucicault	Has Zoe mentioned giving notice at all?
Agnes	I thought you'd paid her.
Boucicault	Paid her, dear? What would I pay her with?
Agnes	You still have the play on, *The Invisible Husband*.
Boucicault	This theatre is dark, Agnes, you passed the notice on your way in, *The Invisible Husband* closed last night.
Agnes	Oh, no . . . I'm so sorry, Dion.
Boucicault	What the public actually wants to see is the Invisible Wife – their very own Fairy Star.
Agnes	Such a stupid title to be given . . .
Boucicault	Nothing less will suffice. She's the darling of the gods, and better yet, of the dress circle. But we aren't going to let them have their Fairy Star until she's strong enough [*Kissing her forehead*] are we, dear?
Agnes	It's only really the touring. If we could remain here just for a while . . .
Boucicault	Not another word, we shall doubtless find some way to survive, like all the poor of New York.
Agnes	One more week, Dion. Then I'll start back, I promise.
Boucicault	Only if you feel up to it, Agnes. Little Eve is frowning at me.
Agnes	I must go, it's time she was in bed.
Boucicault	Goodnight, my child. See you tomorrow.
	[AGNES *exits pushing the baby carriage*]
Patterson	[*As she goes*] But tomorrow I shall be safe on board the packet for Liverpool!
Boucicault	First complication. Bloodgood is about to flee with cash in hand, when his bankruptcy is discovered by his rascally clerk Badger. Badger tries blackmail. Bloodgood tries bribery.
	[PATTERSON *continues doing* BLOODGOOD's *lines, whilst* BOUCICAULT *takes on the role of* BADGER]
Patterson	Mr Badger!
Boucicault	Mr Bloodgood!
Patterson	I have been deceived in you. I confess I did not know your value.

Boucicault	Patience and perseverance, sir, tells in the long run.
Patterson	Here are three thousand dollars – I present them to you for your services.
Boucicault	Further complication. An old seadog called Fairweather has that very day deposited his life's savings, one hundred thousand dollars in cash, in Bloodgood's safekeeping. He now bursts in upon them . . .

[*Enter* FAIRWEATHER]

    . . . having heard rumours that Bloodgood's bank is about to crash, demands the return of his money, and thereupon keels over in a fit of apoplexy.

| Fairweather | [*Keeling over*] I am suffocating – some air – I cannot see – everything is black before my eyes. Am I dying? O, no! no! it cannot be. Some water – quick! Come to me – my wife – my children! Where are they that I cannot fold them in my arms? [*He looks strangely and fearfully into the face of* BLOODGOOD *for an instant, and then breaks into a loud sob*] Oh, my children – my poor, poor little children! |

[*After some convulsive efforts to speak, his eyes become fixed*]

Patterson	Someone run for help. Badger, a doctor, quick.
Boucicault	[*Standing over* FAIRWEATHER] All right, sir, I have studied medicine – that is how I learned most of my loose habits. [*Examines the Captain's pulse and eyes*] It is useless, sir. He is dead.
Patterson	Dead! Can it be possible?

[BOUCICAULT/BADGER *tears open the captain's vest and the receipt for the money falls to the ground*]

Boucicault	His heart has ceased to beat – apoplexy – the causes natural, over-excitement and sudden emotion.
Patterson	Dead!
Boucicault	You are spared the agony of counting out his money.
Patterson	[*The cunning realisation*] Dead . . .
Boucicault	[*Spotting the receipt*] Ha! Here is the receipt! Signed by Bloodgood. As a general rule, never destroy a receipt – there is no knowing when it may yet prove useful. [*Pockets it; then, in his own voice*] They remove the Captain's body to the street . . . [*Gestures impatiently at* PATTERSON, *who drags*

FAIRWEATHER *offstage*] . . . they then disappear about their business. So much for Act One. Acts Two and Three, assorted pathos and romance amongst Bloodgood's victims – and so to Act Four. Badger reappears as a reformed character, at last prepared to expose Bloodgood by means of the receipt – which he has carefully hidden under the floorboards of his tenement room. Unable to find it but determined to destroy it, Bloodgood resorts to desperate measures – he sets fire to the entire house. And thereby creates an absolute sensation.

[*Behind the back wall and before our startled eyes, the scene unfolds in the way that* BOUCICAULT *imagines it will*]

Boucicault   Stage dark. The exterior of the tenement house, 19½ Cross Street. Through the upstairs shutters, the light of a flame can be seen, rising, dying down, reviving. The door is cautiously opened. Bloodgood lets himself out.

[PATTERSON / BLOODGOOD *emerges from the door*]

Patterson   In a few hours, this accursed house will be in ruins. The receipt is concealed there – and it will be consumed in the flames!

Boucicault   The glow of the fire is seen to spread from room to room . . .

Patterson   Now, Badger – do your worst – I am safe! [*He exits*]

Boucicault   The house is gradually enveloped in fire . . .

[*Music*]

[*The fire begins to crackle and roar. Cries from off – "Fire! Fire!" as an alarm is sounded*]

[*Several citizens rush on and mill about in agitation, watching helplessly as the fire spreads*]

[BOUCICAULT / BADGER *pushes his way through them, kicks in a ground-floor window, climbs in and disappears. A young* ONLOOKER *rushes after him*]

Onlooker   Stop! Stop!

[*The* ONLOOKER *leaps through the window, but soon re-appears, face black with smoke, coughing; He collapses into another citizen's arms*]

[*The shutters on an upper window fall to the ground and reveal* BOUCICAULT / BADGER *struggling through the flames on the landing; but there is a loud crash and he disappears from view, as though falling with the inside of the building. The onlookers cry out in horror*]

[BOUCICAULT/BADGER, *dragging himself from the ruins, falls out across the ground-floor window sill. Two of the onlookers, recoiling from the heat, pull him clear. He holds aloft the receipt in triumph: Tableau*]

[*The fire fades away*]

[*Everything goes to blackout as the music ends*]

[*A single match is struck,* BOUCICAULT *lights a cigar. The lights slowly come up again on him and* PATTERSON, *who has sidled back on*]

Boucicault	So there it was. I had secured an audience. That was what it took, in the new age, in the new world. Creating the illusion of fire in a crowded theatre.
Patterson	Hot stuff, Boosy.
Boucicault	They got their money's worth. I went on to invent fireproof scenery, as it happens.
Patterson	There was nobody, you might say, who could hold a candle to you. You were a second Dr Dionysius Lardner!
Boucicault	Lardner's dead and gone and bad cess to his memory, it has nothing further to do with me.
Patterson	All that trickery . . . you took after him as a wizard of applied science, amongst other things.
Boucicault	I was an artist obliged to use whatever tools there were to hand, you think I can't tell the difference between poetry and hokum?
Patterson	Search me.
Boucicault	The theatres of the day were chock full of guano, by public demand. I was obliged to shovel it in, along with all the rest of them, fine – but there was a crucial difference between my dung and theirs, which is why it made more money than anybody else's – my dung had more integrity.
Patterson	It was universally acknowledged as the genuine article.
Boucicault	Listen to me, Patterson. Latent in every age there is a Homer, Virgil or Dante. The question is whether the age desires to draw them forth or not. The Victorian Age has higher

aspirations than these — it demands that Michelangelo market a cheaper sewing machine, it obliges William Shakespeare to write for some scurrilous daily rag!

Patterson   Won't wash, Boosy, them was the boys that rose up above their times, instead of bowing and scraping and pandering . . .

Boucicault   I confronted the major issues of the day!

Patterson   Such as?

Boucicault   The Indian Mutiny, for one.

Patterson   That was good for a laugh.

Boucicault   Negro slavery for another.

Patterson   What was your view of it?

Boucicault   I was against it.

Patterson   Africa salutes you.

Boucicault   You think that was easy, in America, on the eve of the Civil War, to stage a play with a slave heroine?

Patterson   It did you no harm at the box office anyhow.

Boucicault   I knew in my bones the meaning of enslavement and dispossession, I carried the stigmata of a supposed child of nature, of an artist amongst the barbarians, of a licensed song and dance man for the British Empire, that was why I gambled everything on that play! Every cent I'd earned had been spent on the Winter Garden Theatre, I'd only opened it two months previously, if *The Octoroon* had failed I would have gone under . . .

Patterson   So that was why you ended it with the paddle steamer on stage blowing up and burning away to blazes?

Boucicault   What of it?

Patterson   You were a right little pyromaniac, weren't you?

Boucicault   I engineered sensations. There had to be a sensation scene, every time, public demand, the beast was ravenous for it.

Patterson   You see, I was different from you, Boosy, I actually <u>liked</u> the audience.

Boucicault   Up until the night they kicked you to death.

Patterson   I died trying to tell them what they didn't want to hear. You told them all the lies they longed for – in return for which they loved you to death.

Boucicault   It was me who gave the voice of Ireland a hearing on the stages of the world, which it had never before received, in all its tormented history!

Patterson   [*Singing*] Erin, the smile
And the tear in thine eye . . .

Boucicault   I wrote *The Colleen Bawn* and the genial spirit of Oliver Goldsmith danced at last down Broadway with me!

Patterson   Ah, the darlin' Colleen Bawn!

                  [*Music*]

                  [*During the song,* BOUCICAULT *dons the coat, hat and boots of Myles-Na-Coppaleen, lovable rascal and comic hero of* The Colleen Bawn]

Patterson   [*Singing*] Oh, if I was the Emperor of Russia to command,
Or Julius Caesar, or the Lord Lieutenant of the Land,
I'd give up all my wealth, my means, I'd give up my army,
Both the horse, the foot, and the Royal Artillery;
I'd give the crown from off my head, the people on their knees,
I'd give my fleet of sailing ships upon the briny seas,
And a beggar I'd go to sleep, a happy man at dawn,
If by my side, fast for my bride,
I'd the darlin' Colleen Bawn!

                  [*Music ends*]

                  [BOUCICAULT *steps forward with a prop whiskey barrel on his shoulder and addresses the house as* MYLES-NA-COPPALEEN]

Myles   Long life to yez all!

                  [PATTERSON *steps smartly into the role of* CORRIGAN, *a conniving attorney*]

Corrigan   Who's there? Why, 'tis that poaching scoundrel, that horse stealer, Myles-na-Coppaleen – with a keg of illicit whiskey, as bould as Nebuckadezzar. [*Approaching* BOUCICAULT] Is it yourself, Myles?

Myles   No – it's my brother.

Corrigan   What's that on your shoulder?

Myles	It's a bolster belonging to my mother's feather bed.
Corrigan	Stuffed with whiskey?
Myles	How would I know what it's stuffed with? I'm not an upholsterer.
Corrigan	Come now, Myles, I am not the mean creature you imagine.
Myles	Ain't you now, sir? Still, you keep up appearances mighty well, just the same.
Corrigan	I am not that blackguard I have been represented.
Myles	I see your true character, sir — you're another sort of blackguard entirely.
Corrigan	Myles, you have come down in the world lately — and it's the love of Eily O'Connor that's in it — it's the pride of Garryowen that took your heart away, and made you what you are — a smuggler and a poacher.
Myles	Oh, murder — Eily, aroon, why wasn't ye twins, and I could have one of ye, only nature couldn't make two like ye — it would be onreasonable to ax it.

[AGNES *appears, in the role of* EILY O'CONNOR, *accompanied by* HARDRESS CREGAN, EILY's *secret husband in* The Colleen Bawn]

Eily	Poor Myles, do you love me still so much?
Myles	Eily, if tears were poison to the grass, there wouldn't be a green blade on Glenna Hill this day.
Eily	Myles, you saved my life — it belongs to you. There's my hand, what will you do with it.

[MYLES *takes* HARDRESS's *hand and clasps it together with* EILY's]

Myles	Take her, wid all my heart.

[*Tableau. A resounding fanfare*]

[PATTERSON *becomes the master of ceremonies once again*]

Patterson	Her Royal Highness The Queen Victoria And Her Consort The Crown Prince Albert, who's knocking at death's door, so keep it bright and keep it brief!

[*Fanfare again*]

[*Enter the forty-one-year-old* QUEEN VICTORIA *followed by* PRINCE ALBERT, *who is indeed terminally ill*]

Queen   Well, Mr Boucicault – we have seen your play three times now, and we have enjoyed it as much as ever.

Boucicault   Indeed, ma'am, we are thrice blessed.

Queen   You show us our Irish subjects in the manner that renders them the most beloved to us.

[BOUCICAULT *addresses* PRINCE ALBERT *in* MYLES-NA-COPPALEEN's *voice*]

Boucicault   Ach, sir, it's a shamrock itself ye have got; and like that flower she'll come up every year fresh and green fornent ye. When ye cease to love her may dying become ye, and when you <u>do</u> die, leave your money to the poor, your widow to me, and we'll both forgive ye.

[*A shocked silence; defused by the* QUEEN]

Queen   Oh, wait, I believe I can recall it . . . [*Taking* EILY's *lines from the play*] I'm only a poor simple girl, and it's frightened I am to be surrounded by so many . . .

Hardress Cregan   Friends, Eily, friends . . . er, your majesty . . .

Queen   Oh, if I could think so – if I could hope that I had established myself in a little corner of their hearts, there wouldn't be a happier girl alive than the Colleen Bawn!

[BOUCICAULT, AGNES *and* HARDRESS CREGAN *applaud*]

[PRINCE ALBERT *steps aside a little, mopping his brow. He sways unsteadily and reaches out an arm, which* BOUCICAULT *catches*]

Queen   Albert, dearest . . .

Albert   Nothing at all, don't worry, I am not used to such bright lights . . .

Boucicault   [MYLES *again*] Sure, it's only heavy you are, sir, like my own hogshead of poteen there – but you only want tapping for pure spirits to flow out spontaneously, perhaps.

Albert   Perhaps, yes, it is known as the water of life after all, is it not?

Queen   Allow us to congratulate you all once more, and to wish you continued success.

[*And she exits, looking anxiously at* ALBERT, *who wearily follows her off*]

[PATTERSON *ushers* HARDRESS CREGAN *off behind them, and then resumes his footman post*]

[BOUCICAULT *meanwhile is removing his* MYLES-NA-COPPALEEN *outfit*]

Agnes   Dion – you make far too free with her, playing the fool like that.

Boucicault   I am her fool. I have the royal licence.

Agnes   You were playing the Vampire the last time she praised you, but it didn't mean you could sink your teeth in her neck.

Boucicault   Myles-na-Coppaleen has stronger teeth than any vampire, Agnes. This age has made a mockery of all my aspirations . . . at long last I realise that mockery is my own best friend. No limits to what it can achieve, judiciously applied. We are clearly going to be playing this piece for some considerable time.

Agnes   I never dreamt we would ever return home to such acclaim!

Boucicault   I bought a house today, by the way.

Agnes   We don't need a house here, Dion, we already own two houses in New York.

Boucicault   England denied my star its rightful ascendancy . . . I have returned to London for one reason only, to claim my just inheritance by force.

Agnes   Where is it?

Boucicault   The Brompton Road, it's one of a pair of mansions . . . I bought the other one as well, actually, but purely as an investment, shall we dance?

[*Waltz music*]

[BOUCICAULT *sweeps* AGNES *into the dance, as a glittering candelabra appears above their heads*]

[BENJAMIN WEBSTER *enters*]

Patterson   Mr Benjamin Webster!

[*The music stops*]

Agnes   Mr Webster!

Webster   My dear Agnes.

Agnes   Do please excuse me, I really must go and change.

Webster   Of course.

[AGNES *exits*]

Webster	As for you, Dion, you never really change, do you?
Boucicault	All the time, Benjamin. At the behest of the age, I constantly seek to improve myself.
Webster	Entirely at the expense of others.
Boucicault	How else?
Webster	Specifically at the expense of me.
Boucicault	Market forces, Benjamin. Personally, I subscribe to the Free Trade League.
Webster	You dare patronise me . . .
Boucicault	Do I? It's more than you ever did for me, patronage was a thing of the past, according to you – the artist must make his own way, on the open market, very well, I'm making a killing my own way, Webster, congratulate me.
Webster	The Adelphi Theatre is still mine! You have no right to make me a stranger in my own house – you already control the entire creative enterprise, you get half my profits, plus your existing fees, and now to cap it all, these damned royalty payments!
Boucicault	In return for which you are guaranteed capacity houses for *The Colleen Bawn* into the forseeable future.
Webster	On the assumption that you even bother to honour our agreement.
Boucicault	But Benjamin – you and I are men of honour.
	[CHARLES MATTHEWS *and* MADAME VESTRIS *enter*]
Patterson	Mr Charles Matthews and Madame Vestris!
	[*Waltz Music*]
	[BOUCICAULT *dances with* VESTRIS. CHARLES MATTHEWS *and* BENJAMIN WEBSTER *stroll off together*]
	[*The music stops*]
Vestris	Your new house is a monument to your taste and accomplishments, Dion.
Boucicault	Madame is kind.
Vestris	And I gather that you are building a theatre to match?
Boucicault	That will come in due course. Meanwhile, I have taken a lease on Astley's Amphitheatre.

Vestris	Astley's? You are surely not forsaking us for the circus?
	[PATTERSON *sniggers.* BOUCICAULT *shoots him a look*]
Boucicault	I am converting the building into a legitimate theatre.
Vestris	What a charming idea. A theatre in the middle of Lambeth Marsh!
Patterson	Mrs Anne Boursiquot!
	[*Waltz Music*]
	[VESTRIS *sweeps off, as* BOUCICAULT *greets his* MOTHER *and leads her into the dance*]
	[*The music stops abruptly*]
Anne	An overgrown headstrong schoolboy, who has yet to learn the meaning of manhood.
Boucicault	What would you know about that, you surrendered your will into the power of a spider and a swindler.
Anne	I loved a man, it is love itself that you are incapable of!
Boucicault	You made yourself a slave, I will not live like that, mother – I am going to be master of my own fate, however hard they try to ensnare and cage me!
Anne	Poor Mr Webster turned his whole theatre over to you – and all the thanks he gets is to be dragged through the courts of law. It's time you remembered your place.
Boucicault	My place is in history and posterity, those are the only gods I acknowledge, and neither of them will give a tinker's curse for Mr Webster.
Anne	The one and only god you know is money – and you're throwing it to the four winds regardless.
Boucicault	I am in the process of creating a great new London playhouse – the Theatre Royal, Westminster.
Anne	Even I know it's not in Westminster, Dion – it's on Lambeth Marsh.
Boucicault	It is a matter of yards across the river.
Anne	You can maybe adapt other people's plays – but even you cannot rewrite the geography of London!
	[*And she flounces out*]

Patterson   Mr and Mrs George Jordan!

                      [*Waltz music*]

                      [EMILY JORDAN, *a young actress in* BOUCICAULT*'s company, enters with her husband* GEORGE]

                      [BOUCICAULT *sweeps her tempestuously into the dance.* GEORGE JORDAN *watches them for a bit, stiff with suspicion. Then he turns on his heel and strides off*]

                      [*The Candelabra disappears from view, whilst two freestanding apartment doors as in a mansion block of flats, are positioned upstage by* PATTERSON]

                      [BOUCICAULT *and* EMILY JORDAN *continue waltzing together as the lights dim*]

                      [*When the music stops, they kiss*]

Emily   You took so long.

Boucicault   Espionage.

Emily   George has always suspected his own shadow.

Boucicault   There is a way to get rid of shadows. Extinguish all the lights.

Emily   But Dion . . . we shall be entirely in the dark.

Boucicault   So will he, with any luck.

                      [*They disappear through the right-hand door*]

                      [*After a moment, loud knocking is heard from off*]

                      [*The landlady –* MRS BECHSTEIN – *appears, and crosses towards the noise*]

Mrs Bechstein   We have ears, we come, please to leave a little paint on the door . . .

                      [*She is off*]

                      [*The right hand door re-opens, and the heads of* EMILY JORDAN *nad* BOUCICAULT *pop nervously out*]

Emily   Oh my God, he has tracked us down.

Boucicault   I will not be condemned to inhabit a farce!

Patterson   It's a bit late in the day to be saying that.

Emily   Dion, quickly, where can you hide?

Patterson   You mean you have no piano?

[BOUCICAULT *goes calmly to the left-hand door, tries it – it opens*]

Boucicault   Whose apartment is this?

Emily   Colonel Gibbon's.

Boucicault   Au revoir. [*And he disappears through the door*]

Emily   Dion! Ah!

[*The altercation from offstage is reaching a peak*]

[EMILY *slips back in behind her own door just as her husband strides onstage, with* MRS BECHSTEIN *in his wake*]

Jordan   Which is her door, woman?

Mrs Bechstein   Please to wait in lobby pending announcement.

[JORDAN *hammers on the left-hand door*]

Jordan   Emily!

[MRS BECHSTEIN *gives a genteel tap on* EMILY's *door*]

Mrs Bechstein   Please to remember you are now in Mayfair and try to act like gentleman.

[EMILY *opens her door*]

Emily   Why, Mrs Bechstein, what on earth is all the commotion . . . [*Seeing* JORDAN] So it is you. Leave here at once.

Jordan   Bring him out here. [*Shouting past her*] Boucicault!

Emily   Nothing further remains to be said between us, George . . .

[*And she makes to close the door, but he forces it open, thrusts her aside and storms on in*] . . . aah! Mrs Bechstein – this ruffian is a violent former husband of mine, kindly summon the constabulary.

Mrs Bechstein   Police? I do not like, in my house.

Emily   I see, you would much prefer a murder enquiry . . .

Mrs Bechstein   I go.

[*As* MRS BECHSTEIN *hurries off, she passes* COLONEL GIBBON – *in his full ceremonials – entering*]

Gibbon   Evening, Mrs Bluthner.

[*He approaches his front door*]

Emily   [*Leaping to intercept him*] Colonel Gibbon!

Gibbon   Madam . . . don't believe I've had the um . . .

Emily   Emily Thorne. Miss. I'm your new neighbour, Colonel.

Gibbon   I say. How'd do.

Emily   Tell me . . . how is your regiment keeping? These days?

Gibbon   [*At a loss*] Well now . . . by jove . . .

                [JORDAN *bursts back through through* EMILY's *door*]

Jordan   He will not elude me, I saw him enter this whorehouse with
                my bare eyes, bring the despicable kite before me!

Emily   [*Drawing the* COLONEL *aside*] An intruder in our midst, Colonel,
                never mind, a constable has been summoned . . .

                [JORDAN's *eye falls on* COLONEL GIBBON's *door*]

Jordan   He is in there!

                [*He tries to open the* COLONEL's *door, but* BOUCICAULT *has prudently
                locked it from the inside*]

Jordan   Who has the key?

Gibbon   Confound it, sir, that door is mine.

Jordan   Open it.

Gibbon   [*To* EMILY] Are you acquainted with this fellow?

Jordan   There is a contemptible fugitive from the laws of God and
                man cowering behind that door, and I intend to bring him to
                justice!

Gibbon   [*Again to* EMILY] Is he a lunatic?

Eily   Yes I am and yes he is!

Gibbon   [*Turning to* JORDAN] Come along, my man. Be off with you.

Jordan   Are you going to unlock that door?

Gibbon   You heard me. Remove yourself from this house.

                [JORDAN *grabs him by the throat*]

Jordan   [*Shaking him*] GIVE – ME – THE – KEY!

                [*Music, to which the ensuing routine is choreographed*]

                [EMILY *screams as the two men grapple with each other and stagger
                back and forth*]

                [JORDAN *succeeds in toppling* COLONEL GIBBON *to the ground*]

[MRS BECHSTEIN *re-enters with* PATTERSON — *wearing a police constable's helmet — in tow. He hauls* JORDAN *off the* COLONEL, *who is helped up and dusted down by* EMILY *and the* LANDLADY. *While they are all thus diverted,* BOUCICAULT *slips out from behind the* COLONEL's *door and back in through* EMILY's *unnoticed*]

[JORDAN *expostulates with the* CONSTABLE (PATTERSON), *stating his case, the* CONSTABLE *tries* COLONEL GIBBON's *door — which now of course opens — and leads the rest of them through it, to check out* JORDAN's *accusations*]

[BOUCICAULT *re-emerges from behind* EMILY's *door, and slips into the shadows in a downstage corner*]

[*The others pour out through the* COLONEL's *door again, and off — the* CONSTABLE *frogmarching a protesting* JORDAN, EMILY *flirtatiously arm in arm with a delighted* COLONEL GIBBON, *and* MRS BECHSTEIN *plodding along complainingly in the rear*]

[PATTERSON *chucks* JORDAN *into the wings and throws the police constable's helmet after him, then turns back towards* BOUCICAULT *as the music ends*]

Patterson	Nicely played, Boosy. Shame it all had to come out in court, though, wasn't it?

[*And he sets about removing the two apartment doors*]

Boucicault	The whole thrupenny scandal was deliberately trumped up in order to discredit my name.
Patterson	No easy task.
Boucicault	They ganged up, same as ever, to force me out of the business. The men of honour, propriety and decorum saw to it that my Theatre Royal in Westminster was shunned.
Patterson	Oh, yeah — the circus ring down Lambeth way, you mean?
Boucicault	I was declared bankrupt.
Patterson	Not again.
Boucicault	Dispossessed, my theatre and house sold to the highest bidder, driven back out into the provinces like an outlaw . . . but I hadn't forgotten New York. Badger and Bloodgood. If a sensation drama could draw a credulous rabble in one city, why not in another? If *The Poor Of New York* — why not *The Poor Of Liverpool?*
Patterson	Tomorrow Liverpool will ring from Williamson Square to the Pierhead with the news — Bloodgood has absconded . . .

Boucicault   If Liverpool, why not Leeds or Hull, or Glasgow? I sowed
my dragon's teeth the length and breadth of Britain, every
city clamouring in half-witted support of its own local
sensation, *The Poor of Newcastle, The Poor Of Bristol* . . .
until the honourable ranks of the West End managers finally
burst asunder, in a mad scramble for the rights. I re-did the
wretched farrago one final time, as *The Streets of London* . . .
they flocked to it in droves. The burning down of Badger's
hovel had set the entire nation on fire!

Patterson   You know what it is, Boosy — you are a walking testimonial
to those values which have made our Victorian Age a golden
one — plunder, greed, hypocrisy, cynicism, pious self-
righteousness . . .

Boucicault   I played the hand they dealt me, and the little power I earned
from it was applied to the service of my own people!

Patterson   Yourself and your mother, you mean?

Boucicault   I have done far more in the Irish cause than ever you
achieved, you footling little balladmonger, I wrote "Arrah-na-
Pogue", and I wrote "The Wearing Of The Green" to go with
it, the very anthem of the National movement!

Patterson   [*Sings*] Oh, Paddy dear! an' did you hear
The news that's going round?
The shamrock is by law forbid
To grow on Irish ground . . .

Boucicault   I insisted that the world premiere of that play be given in
Dublin!

Patterson   [*Sings*] St Patrick's Day no more we'll keep
His colours can't be seen,
For there's a cruel law agin
The wearing of the green . . .

Boucicault   They cheered me through the streets after it, two other
theatres were staging *The Colleen Bawn* simultaneously, as a
tribute!

Patterson   [*Sings*] She's the most distressful country
That ever yet was seen,
For they're hanging men and women there
For wearin' of the green.

[*Speaks*] Sure that's an ould song that everybody knows, you
learnt it from your ma.

Boucicault	The tune I may have learnt, the words I wrote myself.
Patterson	Re-wrote, you mean.
Boucicault	They are my words!
Patterson	You and your work have the one thing in common – dubious paternity.
Boucicault	I gave benefits, all over the country, to raise money for the Fenian prisoners' families. There was a bomb went off outside Clerkenwell prison . . .
Patterson	Twelve dead, a hundred and twenty injured.
Boucicault	I deplored it. Even so, after it happened, "The Wearing Of The Green" was forbidden to be sung anywhere in the British Empire.
Patterson	You were thrilled to bits about that, weren't you? I'll tell you what it really is, Boosy – you love to play the poacher – so long as you're still officially the gamekeeper.
Boucicault	It was I who challenged Disraeli to release the Fenian prisoners!
Patterson	Yeah – after you'd finalised arrangements to become an American citizen. You heard what Dizzy said when they showed him your letter? "Boucicault? Boucicault? Where have I heard that name before? Is it someone in the conjuring business?"
Boucicault	He has had leisure since to regret his condescension.
Patterson	Sure, what of it? Didn't you get your free publicity?
Boucicault	It was no stunt! Many times I went to the Houses of Parliament to consult with members of the Irish Party. It was made very clear to me that should I wish to volunteer my services, I could choose my own constituency.
Patterson	By God, that would have turned the trick all right – Conn the Shaughraun, at the dispatch box – speaking in support of Charles Stewart Parnell! [*Doing* CONN] "Long life to yer honours, and isn't it a grand thing for a tatterdemalion the likes of my poor self to be addressin' all you fine English gentlemen? I freely confess I nivir did an honest day's work in my life before this – but drinkin' and fishin' and shootin' and sportin' and love-makin' – sure it's the House of Lords I belong in by rights! Beggin' your pardons . . . "

Boucicault	I can understand your bitterness. The same people who slaughtered you showered me with honours.
Patterson	Sure, why wouldn't they? You flattered the daylights out of them, with your silver-tongued charming peasant rascals, and all their winning, wheedling, conniving ways . . . your colonial soul discovered its strength in fraudulence and deceit, Dizzy had you right, you were in the conjuring business, you conjured up a never-never emerald island, fake heroics and mettlesome beauties and villains made of pasteboard, outwitted through eternity by the bogus grinning peasant rogue as only you could play him – with the blather and codology and the gaslight moonshine.
Boucicault	People need laughter and lyricism, reassurance, why not? – a sweet dream to drive out the nightmares, who the blazes are you to talk, you offered them the same thing!

[PATTERSON *slowly smiles*]

Patterson	There you are, now. You and me both. Paddy the Clown. Will we call it a day?
Boucicault	NO!

[*He falls to his knees*]

Patterson	Only a matter of time, old fella. You were already fifty-five when you wrote *The Shaughraun*, don't forget.

[*He has fetched a tin of white powder from the make-up box, and he stands behind the kneeling* BOUCICAULT *and whitens his remaining hair during the following*]

Patterson	That was your last real success, now, am I right?
Boucicault	I have plays in me still.
Patterson	They're all agreed you've outlived your time.
Boucicault	They're saying my mind has gone, that I'm senile, any scurrilous damnable lie to try and force me under for the last time, I won't submit. I have never stopped writing.
Patterson	You don't think you've maybe penned enough of them plays by now? How many is it anyhow? Any advance on two hundred?
Boucicault	It's of no importance, only the work matters, I am no Conn the Shaughraun, I have worked every day of my life and most nights, work is the one thing that gives this life an illusion of meaning . . .

Patterson	Except for marriage, of course.

[BOUCICAULT *stiffens, clambers to his feet*]

Patterson	Agnes appeared in *The Shaughraun* with you, I take it?
Boucicault	For a spell, she did.

[AGNES *enters, dressed as* MOYA – *the simple peasant girl who is* CONN's *beloved in* The Shaugraun – *and carrying a bunch of wild flowers*]

Agnes	Ah! Conn, do you see those flowers? I picked them by the wayside as I came along, and I put them in my breast. They are dead already. The life and fragrance have gone out of them. Killed by the heat of my heart. So it may be with you, since I picked you and put you there. Won't the life go out of your love? Hadn't I better leave you where you are?
Patterson	Twenty-five years of faithful marriage to you. Six children she gave you, and working throughout it all, playing every role you demanded of her, trailing after you all over the map.
Boucicault	She didn't go unrewarded.
Patterson	Watching you, truffling away under the skirt of every new young actress in the company, that was her reward, you mangy old goathead. Dionysius Lardner rides again.
Anne	Dion . . .
Boucicault	All right! Enough! Go home, Agnes. It's over.

[AGNES *tosses the flowers aside and pulls off the Moya shawl*]

Agnes	I no longer remember even which mistress it was . . . one of the passing fancies, clearly, not one that you actually lived with, there were such a lot it's hard to recall it now . . . you bought her a cottage in Kent, I think, and a rather hideous jardiniere, made from streaky green marble, I remember the jardiniere, you see, because for some extraordinary reason it was just then that it all finally died for me. So you needn't any longer fear that I am going to cling on and beg and plead for you to respect me as your wife, yet again . . . I barely even remember what being loved by you felt like. However – we do still have children, Dion, and I do not consider it kind to them for their father to be living with other women three thousand miles away . . . so. Since at least the geography is surmountable, I suggest that I bring them here to New York to live. Or else that you return to London.

Boucicault   You are free to run your own life, so will they be soon enough, kindly allow me to get on with mine.

Agnes   Free . . . you're not free, never can be free, Dion. You've spent your whole career pitting yourself against the Age, fulminating against it . . . when all the time the savagery of the Age was concentrated in you, every life you have ever touched has been a victim of it, sacrificed on the altar of your work . . . but surely know your plays will amount to little more than breaking wind in a stiff breeze, at the end of all, that your last and worst victim is you yourself, Dion? Because the truth is, you _are_ the Age. It's all there is to you.

Boucicault   How much do you need?

Agnes   One thousand seven hundred and fifty dollars, for the moment.

Boucicault   Precise as ever.

Agnes   I have two of the girls with me, as you're well aware, it's the cost of transporting us all back to London.

Boucicault   Cheap at the price. Here, take it.

                   [_Giving her the money_]

Agnes   Thank you, Dion. I gather your new play is expected to flop, yet again. We'll be thinking of you.

                   [_She exits_]

Patterson   The new flop in question being entitled – what else – _The Jilt_! In which Myles O'Hara, an ageing bohemian jockey and gentleman of the turf, arrives at The Abbots, the ancestral home of Sir Buddleigh Woodstock and his pretty young sister Kitty.

                   [_The backdrop parts, to reveal_ MARCUS WYLIE, _the villain, alone with_ KITTY WOODSTOCK, _the heroine._

Wylie   Kitty – can I do nothing to please you?

Kitty   I will tell you what <u>not</u> to do, Sir Marcus. Don't follow me about with a box of sweets as children try to catch birds by putting a piece of salt on their tails. If ever I do fall in love, I must plunge into it unawares – and before I know where I am.

                   [_She is striding off, and runs straight into the arms of_ BOUCICAULT, _who has entered the scene in the character of_ MYLES O'HARA]

Kitty	Oh!
O'Hara	For what we have received, may the Lord make us truly thankful.
Kitty	I beg your pardon, sir. [*And she makes her way off*]
Wylie	You present yourself without much ceremony.
O'Hara	Egad, sir, it was the most delightful ceremony I ever encountered. [*Offering card, which* WYLIE *takes*]
Wylie	Myles O'Hara? I beg your pardon. Your name is so celebrated that I feel we are already acquainted. I shall tell Sir Buddleigh of your arrival.

[*He exits*]

Patterson	The part of Kitty Woodstock having been written for that vivacious young newcomer, Miss Louise Thorndyke, who will now afford us a foretaste of the thrilling denouement!

[LOUISE THORNDYKE – KITTY WOODSTOCK – *re-enters, and addresses* BOUCICAULT]

Kitty	Mr O'Hara, I cannot quite understand you. Do you know that you are the only man that has been received here who has never made love to me?
O'Hara	Good heavens, Miss Woodstock! What d'you take me for? Do you think I should mistake myself so far? You know who and what I am.
Kitty	I think so.
O'Hara	And who and what you are. Think of the extreme distance between us.
Kitty	Extremes meet sometimes.
O'Hara	I am a poor broken-down adventurer, penniless, homeless – a bohemian in the city, a vagabond in the shires, I am a tramp that stops at your gate, and takes a hungry look at you through the bars.
Kitty	So you are going to leave us?
O'Hara	And I leave my life here.
Kitty	In the stable with your horse?
O'Hara	No! at your feet. I can't help it. Your eyes wring it out of my soul. I must speak or die.

Kitty	Then speak for heaven's sake.
O'Hara	I may offend you.
Kitty	The only offence has been your silence.
O'Hara	My love . . .
Kitty	Yes, yours.
	[*He kisses her*]
Patterson	Pardon me for butting in, but what theatre is this exactly?
Boucicault	The Theatre Royal, Sydney.
Patterson	Sydney?
Boucicault	We took the play on a tour across Australia. It was in Sydney that Louise and I were married. [*Taking her hand*]
Patterson	You mean . . . on top of everything else you've become a bigamist?
Boucicault	NO! [*To* LOUISE] It's not so.
	[LOUISE *smiles at him, and exits*]
	[BOUCICAULT *steps downstage as the backdrop closes*]
Boucicault	The supposed marriage between Agnes Robertson and myself had never legally existed.
Patterson	So. You were ready and willing to reduce your wife to a harlot in the eyes of society, and to see your children illegitimised and disinherited – the very grievances you yourself have been whingeing about all morning?
Boucicault	There was none of that, it was all just words and pieces of paper!
Patterson	What else is your entire life?
Boucicault	I needed to marry Louise!
Patterson	You were sixty-five.
Boucicault	Sixty-four.
Patterson	She was twenty-one!
Boucicault	I had to start over again, cut all the strings, can't you understand? I had played by their rules, the whole time, I had to master my own fate, once and for all, in the teeth of all their hollow gods, I have a multitude of plays in me still!
Patterson	The judge found in favour of Agnes.

Boucicault	Made no odds, Louise and I had a second wedding, here in New York, after the divorce.
Patterson	What about the alimony?
Boucicault	How do they expect me to pay it, I have no money.
Patterson	All them flops.
Boucicault	I do a little teaching – here, in this theatre, the Madison Square, they have started a drama school, it keeps me in touch with the young people which is where I most belong . . . I've just been somewhat tired lately, nothing serious, I think I may have caught something, it's been raining for days now . . .

[PATTERSON *is bringing on a brass bed*]

Boucicault	What are you doing?
Patterson	I'm putting you to bed, Boosy. You don't sound a bit well.

[*He leads* BOUCICAULT *to the bed and pulls back the covers*]

Patterson	Get tucked in there like a good man and I'll sing you a little lullaby.

[BOUCICAULT *gets into the bed, as* PATTERSON *sings quietly*]

Patterson	[*Singing*] I'm very happy where I am Far across the say, I'm very happy far from home In North Amerikay . . .

[*Speaks*] This is one of your own devising, d'you mind it at all?

Boucicault	Why wouldn't I? It's more than a match for any of your come-all-ye's.
Patterson	Sure we're songbirds of a feather, the pair of us.

[*Sings*] It's lonely in the night, when Pat
Is sleeping by my side,
I lie awake and no-one knows
The big tears that I've cried . . .

For a little voice still calls me back
To my far, far countrie,
And nobody can hear it spake,
O, nobody but me . . .

[*Speaks*] Calling you home, Boosy – but sure where is there a home for the likes of you? Apart from centre stage with the bright light on you?

	[*Sings*] There is a certain spot of ground It makes a dawny hill, And from below the voice comes out, I cannot keep it still . . .
Boucicault	[*Starting up feverishly*] NO! I will not go under!
	[LOUISE THORNDYKE *comes running on*]
Louise	Dion, dearest, it's all right . . .
Boucicault	I am not yet ready to go!
Louise	There's no need, you're not well, they're not expecting you to go.
Boucicault	[*Looking at her amazed*] What are you talking about?
Louise	The theatre school, of course.
	[BOUCICAULT *gives vent to a harsh laugh*]
Louise	Your students have sent you crocuses and lilies.
Boucicault	Have they indeed, kindly inform them they're a little bit previous with their funeral tributes.
Louise	You know quite well they are very impatient for your return.
Boucicault	Louise . . .
Louise	Yes, darling?
Boucicault	My play – *A Tale Of A Coat* – bad news. It closed at the weekend.
Louise	Hush, it's all right, I know all about that.
Boucicault	For eleven long years they have denied me a success . . . I have written for a monster who forgets.
Louise	You are the greatest man of the theatre in this age, every passer-by in the street knows that.
	[BOUCICAULT *slips out of bed and addresses the house*]
Boucicault	She says you will go bail for me . . . you are the only friend I have. Long life t'ye! – Many a time have you looked over my faults – will you be blind to them now and hould out your hands once more to a poor Shaughraun?
Louise	Dion, please come back to bed.
Boucicault	You know, when I wrote that kind of speech, the older actors were scandalised by it. They were accustomed to exit lines, you see, without them they felt simply stranded on the stage.

They used to say to me, "dear boy, can't you possibly offer me
a few words to take me off, you've left me high and dry . . . "
you see the foolishness of it, Louise, they literally couldn't get
off, couldn't leave the stage, just a few words, all that's needed,
those precious few, so long as they're the right ones, to turn
the trick, the exact few words that'll manage at last please God
to GET ME OFF!

[*He collapses. She rushes over, helps him up and back to the bed*]

Louise   Don't, don't, come on now, I'm putting you back to bed . . .
help me, Dion . . . come along, that's it, you're going to get
well . . .

[*She has manhandled him into bed*]

Darling, I'm going to fetch the doctor now, please just lie
quiet until I get back, all right?

[*She kisses him, walks to the side of the stage*]

I shall only be gone for a moment.

[*She exits*]

Patterson   She had the words to get her off, did you notice?

[*He stands at the head of the bed looking down at* BOUCICAULT, *and
resumes singing the song*]
O, little voice, ye call me back
To my far, far countrie,
And nobody can hear ye speak,
O, nobody but me . . .

[*Speaks*] You've had your day in court now, Boosy. You're
being sent down.

Boucicault   Could we not at least do the wake before we go?

Patterson   You're not getting any wake. You're too high-falutin' now for
that class of a send-off.

Boucicault   Not mine, not my wake – Conn's.

Patterson   Eh?

Boucicault   From *The Shaughraun*. The Wake Scene.

Patterson   Ah, merciful jaysus, not another scene from a play . . .

Boucicault   All the accoutrements are in place, it won't detain you more
than a minute. It was the finest scene of my career.

Patterson   Weren't they all?

Boucicault   The audience knows that Conn is actually alive – but his
                   mother and the neighbours take him for dead, you see . . .

Patterson   I know the gag, just start the bloody music.

                   [*Music: "The Oolaghaun"*]

                   [MRS O'KELLY, CONN's *grieving widowed mother, is helped on by
                   two male mourners. They are followed by the chief keener,* BIDDY
                   MADIGAN. *All of them are carrying bottles and jugs of liquor, and
                   lighted candles, and they are singing the lament for the dead*]

All   Och, Oolaghaun! – och Oolaghaun!
                   Make his bed both wide and deep!
                   Och, Oolaghaun! – och Oolaghaun!
                   He is only gone to sleep.

                   Why did ye die? – oh, why did ye die?
                   And lave us all alone to cry?

Biddy   [*Wailing*] Oh, oh, oho! [*Rocking herself*] The widow had a son –
                   an only son – wail for the widow!

All   [*Singing*] Why did ye die? – Why did ye die?

                   [*They have grouped themselves around the bed:* BOUCICAULT *is once
                   again* CONN THE SHAUGHRAUN]

Biddy   The boy grew strong, for she fed him with her heart's blood. A,
                   hogoola! Where is he now? Cowld in his bed! Why did ye die?

All   [*Singing*] Leaving us to sigh! Och, hone!

Biddy   None was like him – none could compare . . . [*Breaking off: an
                   aside to the nearest mourner,* SULLIVAN] . . . good luck to ye, gimme
                   a drop of somethin' to put the spirit in one, for the fire's gettin'
                   low.

                   [SULLIVAN *hands her a jug of punch*]

Mrs O'Kelly   It's mighty consolin' to hear this . . . Mr Malone, you are not
                   eatin'.

Mourner   No, ma'am, I'm drinkin'. I drink now and again, by way of
                   variety. [*Aside to* SULLIVAN] Biddy is not up to herself.

Sullivan   Oh, wait till she'll rise on the top of that noggin.

                   [BIDDY *has taken a long draught. She now places the jug by the bed
                   and rises again to the occasion*]

Biddy   He was brave! He was brave! He had the heart of a lion and
                   the legs of a fox.

[CONN *picks up the jug, drains it dry, and replaces it, unobserved by the other characters*]

Biddy   His voice was softer than the cuckoo of an evening. and sweeter than the blackbird after a summer shower. Ye colleens, ye will never hear the voice of Conn again! [*She blows her nose*]

Conn   [*To the house*] It's a mighty pleasant thing to die like this, once in a way, and hear all the good things said about ye after ye're dead and gone, when they can do you no good.

Biddy   His name will be the pride of the O'Kellys for evermore!

Conn   I was a big blackguard when I was alive.

Biddy   Noble and beautiful!

Conn   Ah, go on out o' that!

Biddy   [*Picking up her jug*] Oh, he was sweet and strong . . . who the divil's been at my jug of punch?

Mrs O'Kelly   Nobody is drinkin' — yez all despise the occasion!

[*Knocking from without*]

Sullivan   What's that?

[*Enter* CAPTAIN MOLINEUX, *the hapless young English officer in the play*]

Molineux   I don't come to disturb this . . . a . . . melancholy . . . a, entertainment . . . I mean, a . . . this festive solemnity . . .

Mrs O'Kelly   Heaven bless you for coming to admire the last of him. Here he is — isn't he beautiful?

Molineux   [*Aside*] The vagabond is winking at me.

Mrs O'Kelly   How often have I put him to bed as a child, and sung him to sleep! Now he will be put to bed with a shovel, and oh! the song was never sung that will awaken him.

Molineux   If any words could put life into him, I came here to speak them. A reprieve has been granted! A heavenly abode is prepared for him in spite of all!

[*A moment's silence, then they all burst out cheering and carry* MOLINEUX *off on their shoulders*]

Boucicault   [*Sitting up*] I never wrote that. What did he mean?

Patterson   I assume you're still hell-bent on being counted amongst the angels?

Boucicault   Appeal dismissed was the verdict, as I understood it.

Patterson   Ah, I'm prepared to stretch a point. It was a tidy little scene all right, that wake, I'll grant you that.

Boucicault   I could show you more, if you like . . .

Patterson   [*Hastily*] Another time, maybe, we have to see about getting you upstairs. You're being buried from the Church of the Transfiguration, what do you think of that, now?

Boucicault   Will there be a decent turnout?

Patterson   Not bad, for a matinee. Are you ready?

Boucicault   Ready.

Patterson   Good luck, then, Boosy, no hard feelings, nice knowing you.

[PATTERSON *retires with funeral gravity to the side*]

[*Organ music*]

[BOUCICAULT *settles himself in dignified repose*]

[*The backdrop parts to reveal twinkling heavens, with a great central star bearing* BOUCICAULT's *portrait*]

[*The members of the company enter in mourning dress, and lay wreaths and flowers all over the bed*]

[*The bed begins to ascend to heaven*]

[*The mourners doff their hats and fall to their knees. A heavenly choir is heard*]

[*The music and singing build towards a climax, as the levitating* BOUCICAULT *climbs ever more heavenwards, and his star lights up and sparkles*]

[*Suddenly water starts cascading down on the catafalque.* BOUCICAULT *sits up smartly – he is getting drenched*]

[*The music and the heavenly choir stop abruptly*]

Patterson   Ah, holy God, isn't that just typical? The heavens open, and what happens? – the rain comes through the bloody roof!

[*The star and all the other lights flash, crackle, fuse and expire*]

[*Circus music*]

[*Blackout*]

[*The End*]

Pentecost

Pentecost was first performed in the Guildhall, Derry, by the Field Day Theatre Company on 23 September 1987 with the following cast:

Lenny	Stephen Rea
Marian	Eileen Pollock
Lily	Barbara Adair
Ruth	Paula Hamilton
Peter	Jonathan Kent

Director   Patrick Mason
Design   Bunny Christie
Lighting Design   Conleth White

The English premiere was presented by the Tricycle Theatre Company at the Lyric Theatre, Hammersmith, on 9 January 1989 with the following cast:

Lenny	Adrian Dunbar
Marion	Dearbhla Molloy
Ruth	Michelle Fairley
Peter	Sam Dale
Lily	Barbara Adair

Director   Nicolas Kent
Design   Poppy Mitchell
Lighting Design   David Colmer

Act 1

[The time is 1974]

[The place is Belfast]

*[The play takes place in the downstairs back part of a respectable
working-class "parlour" house, built in the early years of this
century. There is a kitchen with a fireplace, a rocking chair, a sofa,
a dining table. On one side a doorway leads into the scullery, with
its flagstone floor and its old cast-iron range for cooking on and its
"jawbox" of a sink. At the far end of the scullery another door leads
into the pantry, which we can't see]*

*[The large kitchen window looks out on the back yard, which is
very narrow, with high, whitewashed walls topped by lines of
broken glass. The yard door is heavily bolted, even though its worn
ribs are showing through]*

*[On the other side of the kitchen is the door leading into the
hall and thence to the rest of the house. There is an under-stairs
cupboard by this door]*

*[There is a single electric light with conical shade hanging from the
middle of the ceiling in kitchen and scullery both; but there are
also working gas mantles in the walls]*

*[Everything is real except the proportions. The rooms are narrow,
but the walls climb up and disappear into the shadows above the
stage. The kitchen in particular is cluttered, almost suffocated,
with the furnishings and bric-a-brac of the first half of the century,
all the original fixtures and fittings still being in place. But in
spite of now being shabby, musty, threadbare, it has all clearly
been the object of a desperate, lifelong struggle for cleanliness,
tidiness, orderliness – godliness]*

*[The people are MARIAN, LENNY and PETER, who are all 33; RUTH, who
is 29; and LILY MATTHEWS, who is 74]*

I

[*A night in February*]

[LENNY *is seated on the kitchen sofa, playing "I Can't Get Started" on his trombone. His tape machine is on the table, providing the rhythm-section backing. He is wearing his overcoat and hat: it's very cold, there is no fire in the grate. Only the single electric lights are on*]

[MARIAN *enters from the hall, also in her overcoat. She switches off* LENNY'*s backing track. His trombone peters out*]

Marian   Did you make tea?

Lenny   The gas is off.

[MARIAN *has moved on into the kitchen, and is peering into a teapot on the top of the range*]

Marian   What's this?

Lenny   That's old. So. What do you reckon?

Marian   There's a cup sitting here with milk and sugar in it. Christ.

Lenny   I told you. I haven't touched a thing.

Marian   She must have brewed this up just before it happened.

Lenny   No such thing.

Marian   She never got a chance to pour it out.

Lenny   The ambulancemen, is all it would have been.

Marian   It's stone cold.

Lenny   The ambulancemen at the door, is all it possibly could have been.

[MARIAN *turns her full attention on him for the first time*]

Marian   I see. They prepared a nice pot of tea, prior to removing the corpse.

Lenny   She walked out of here, in her Sunday hat and coat and best handbag, is what I'm saying, under her own steam, into the ambulance, it was in the hospital she died . . .

Marian   When?

Lenny   How do I know, under the anaesthetic.

Marian   When?

Lenny	Why?
Marian	I'm asking you when.
Lenny	What does it matter, Wednesday sometime . . .
Marian	Christ.
Lenny	Meaning what?
Marian	Why is her family not here?
Lenny	No surviving relatives, I told you. There wasn't even anybody at the funeral.
Marian	So. I wonder how they manage in a case like that.
Lenny	My Great-Aunt Rosaleen owned the whole terrace, it was all in her will, I told . . .
Marian	Holding a funeral when there's nobody at it, I mean.
Lenny	Very good, Marian. Right, well, let's see. The wee butcher from the shop on the front of the road was there, her churchgoing cronies, a few oul' dolls who used to live next door when there used to be a door next door, no family is actually of course what I was saying, okay? Me, I was there. Standing foundered in Dundonald at half nine this morning, being tonguelashed by the Free Presbyterian notion of a requiem mass, that was it. Just what is this?
Marian	You haven't exactly let the grass grow.
Lenny	Just how is this, whenever I start the evening doing you a favour, ten minutes into it and suddenly I'm a heartless creep, dishonouring the dead, I never once clapped eyes on the woman!
Marian	Well you've sure as hell inherited the woman.
Lenny	The house, I've inherited the house, by law it has to come to me once the sitting tenant's dead, you think I ever wanted this? – I thought you'd maybe appreciate the chance, before there's any sort of an auction, you could have the pick of all this for your shop, you were never off my back about being careless with money, okay, great stuff, go ahead and take advantage of it.
Marian	You haven't lost your knack of feeling put-upon, I see.
Lenny	[*Leaping up*] Forget I ever mentioned it, Marian.

Marian	Sit down. Here. Stick this in your gub. [*Producing a half-bottle of brandy from her shoulder-bag*] What was her name?
Lenny	Matthews. Mrs Alfred George Matthews.
Marian	[*A toast*] God love you, Mrs Matthews.
Lenny	Lily to her friends.
Marian	Nice house, Lily, you kept it lovely.

[*She swigs and passes the bottle to* LENNY, *who finally decides to accept it*]

Lenny	Responsibilities, who needs them.
Marian	Property used to be theft, in your book.
Lenny	What are you supposed to do? It was my mother insisted I go to the funeral. "That wee woman lived her whole life in that house, it's your responsibility now, the least you can do is honour her memory" – what memory? None of us even once met her. If she'd known her rent was going' straight to the Legion of Mary, she'd have dropped dead years ago. The last thing she'd ever have asked for was me mooching round her graveside, did it never strike you that funerals and weddings are much of a muchness in this country?
Marian	Certainly. Our wedding was exactly like a funeral.
Lenny	There's just one way to tell the difference. Nobody takes photographs at a funeral.
Marian	Apart from the Special Branch.

[*She has wandered back into the kitchen and is examining a row of mugs displayed on a shelf*]

Look at this. Queen Victoria's Diamond Jubilee, the wedding of Queen Mary, the Coronation of Lizzie the Second, 1953 – that must be the most modern item in the house. Most of the furniture's Edwardian, there's a Regency dressing table upstairs that must have come down through her grandparents.

Lenny	Is it all worth much? What do you reckon?

[MARIAN *deliberates, moving about amongst the furniture*]

Marian	As I remember it – what was the word you most detested in the whole of the English language – "antiques".

Lenny	Yeah. Well. You felt much the same way about "trombone".
Marian	I didn't feel that different about "antiques" as a matter of fact.
Lenny	Antiques have been your whole livelihood.
Marian	It's been my trade, I don't have to love it.
Lenny	You always loved it.
Marian	Things, individually crafted, well-cared-for, those I love, not the business, you never could grasp that. Old and beautiful things.
Lenny	The sash my father wore.
Marian	Up yours too. I've sold the shop. If you want to know.

[LENNY *is thunderstruck*]

Lenny	You've done what?
Marian	For an amazingly good price, when you consider the state the city's in, but then it's what I'm good at, isn't it, as you're at pains to point out, trading, buying and selling. I don't have to love it. Just get on with it. Survival. It's one bloody useful knack, knowing the value of things to people, what they'll pay, what they think they're worth. The things, that is. The people of course are not worth shit. I didn't have to love them either. You and I tend to diverge on that point, you having all that deep-seated compassion, for anything that snuffles into your shoulder . . .
Lenny	Hold on a minute!
Marian	In my case the embattled bourgeoisie of Belfast was one long procession of avaricious gobshites – hell-bent on overloading their lounge cabinets and their display units with any bauble or knick-knack, so long as it looked like it cost more than it did, so long as it was showy enough to advertise their grandeur, and their fashionable taste and stylishness, not to mention their absolutely bottomless vulgarity, it was bad enough before the shooting-match started, it's grotesque at this point, I couldn't handle any more of it.
Lenny	Why Marian did it not maybe, I mean how come you never . . ?
Marian	Besides I didn't have you to feed and clothe any more, so who needs it? Do you ever actually earn money these days?
Lenny	What do you imagine you're going to do?

Marian	You can't possibly get paid for playing that thing.
Lenny	Why did you bother coming here to look at this at all?
Marian	I need a house.
Lenny	You what? What do you mean, a house? You're not thinking of starting up as an estate agent?
Marian	I need a house. To live in.
Lenny	You've got a flat to live in.
Marian	I've put it on the market.
Lenny	Marian . . . Exactly what's going on with you?
Marian	Have you had this place valued?
Lenny	Of course I haven't had it bloody valued, the woman was only buried this morning!
Marian	I'll buy it from you. Wholesale. House and contents, just the way they stand at the minute. The lock, the stock and the barrel. I'll pay you the going price. Whatever the valuation is. We can go and see your solicitor uncle first thing in the morning.

[*In the time that it takes for* LENNY *to get to grips with this bizarre notion, the soft booming of two distant explosions is heard*]

Lenny	What kind of game are we playing here?
Marian	Trading, buying and selling. The one I'm so good at.
Lenny	God. The years I've spent wondering what you'd hit me with next . . .
Marian	I want the house. No joke.
Lenny	Talk sense!
Marian	You haven't lost your belief in the free spirit, surely, the unencumbered impulse. The pure spontaneous gesture. All that life-embracing bollocks that I so conspicuously lacked, well here's me right now acting like mad on impulse, Lenny, free-spirited as all get out, so what exactly are we waiting for?
Lenny	The name of the game, for a start.
Marian	Who cares, imagine whatever takes your fancy, maybe I've noticed a Gainsborough lying behind the mangle, check it out. So long as we have a deal.

Lenny	A deal, Marian – is what we don't actually have. You and me.
Marian	Don't start that.
Lenny	Still don't have, not since a year ago last May.
Marian	Business is all I'm here to talk . . .
Lenny	So fine, you want to buy this hovel for reasons as yet unexplained, that can certainly be arranged – providing we're agreeing to a brand new deal. Namely. The house is yours as stated, terms agreed. In return for a divorce.
Marian	We are divorced, as good as.
Lenny	I'm talking about your signature on a petition.
Marian	What difference does it make?
Lenny	It makes it official, it makes it binding, it makes it definite.
Marian	Not in the one and only place where it actually means something . . .
Lenny	The church? – the church is beneath my notice, it's beneath contempt, if the church won't recognise my divorce, that's fine, great. Because I don't recognise its existence. Because out here in the real world, Marian, we've been conducting separate lives in separate houses for one year ten months, where's the point, it's only suspended animation, I can't keep on like this, let's pull the plug and have done with it. I can't see what your difficulty is. [*She is silent*] There's nobody else I'm planning to marry, if that's what you're thinking. There's nobody else full stop. It's got nothing to do with anybody else. [*She remains silent*] We have no children, we have no mortgage, there's no argument over an estate, you were the one who made all the money anyway, you've got it all, what's your problem? What are you holding out for? We're never going to get together again, not in a million years, you can't stand me, less than ever, why prolong it? Let's get shot of it. What's your objection?

[MARIAN *remains silent for a moment longer, then turns abruptly towards him*]

Marian	Okay. Tomorrow morning. Your uncle can take care of that along with the house.

[LENNY *is gobsmacked*]

Lenny	Well. I'd rather it wasn't actually my Uncle Phelim. I mean, I don't mind, if you want to talk about it . . .

Marian   You've said all there is. I agree.

Lenny   I mean, I'm not trying to force you into a corner. It's
                  something we need to feel the same way about.

Marian   It's settled. We're doing it.

Lenny   Ach, for Jesus' sake come off it, Marian, you can't possibly live
                  in this gaff, it's the last house on the road left inhabited! –
                  the very road itself is scheduled to vanish off the map, it's the
                  middle of a redevelopment zone, not to mention the minor
                  detail that it's slap bang in the firing line, the Prods are all up
                  in that estate, [*Gesturing towards the back of the house*] the Taigs
                  are right in front of us, anyway look at it – it's reeking of damp,
                  there's five different layers of wallpaper hanging off the walls,
                  she was still using gas lamps in half the rooms, nothing to cook
                  on apart from that ancient range, brown lino everywhere and
                  rooms bunged up with junk, there's probably rats, mice and
                  badgers in the belfry, it's riddled with rot and it's dingy, dank
                  and absolutely freezing!

Marian   Perfect. I'll take it.

                  [*She sweeps out into the hall to take another look around.* LENNY
                  *is left staring after her, entirely at a loss for further words. He
                  punches his cassette player on the table and the backing track is
                  heard again. He picks up his trombone and plays along to it*]

                  [*The lights fade slowly to blackout*]

                  [*End of Scene One*]

II

[*A night in April*]

[*The gaslight comes up on* MARIAN *standing in the scullery, making herself a cup of coffee. She is wearing a sweater and skirt. She has lit the kitchen fire as well as the gas mantles*]

[*She carries her coffee into the kitchen and pauses to take a sip of it, gazing into the fire, the flames glimmering over her face*]

[*She sets the coffee down on the table, fetches the half-bottle of brandy from her shoulder bag and unscrews the top*]

Marian Begging your pardon, Lily Matthews. I'm sure no sup ever passed your lips. Show a little mercy. Some of us are made of weaker stuff.

[*She pours a shot of brandy into the coffee, and then carries both over to the rocking chair, sits herself down and rocks a little*]

Pleased to make your acquaintance, by the way.

[*Holding up the coffee and taking a swig, as in a mock toast, and then setting down the coffee on the floor – which causes her to notice a raffia basket tucked in beside the chair. She picks it up, takes the lid off, lifts out a piece of unfinished knitting still on the needles*]

So. What was this going to be?

[*She finds the pattern in the basket*]

Aha. A woolly bedjacket – by God you certainly need one in that bedroom. I might just finish it off for you. If you're sure you don't object to me wearing it, that is.

[*She rocks a little more*]

I've got to make some plans for you and me, Lily Matthews.

[*A low distant rumble of explosions is heard*]

[LILY MATTHEWS, *in Sunday coat and hat and best handbag, appears in the shadowy doorway leading from the pantry*]

Lily I don't want you in my house.

[MARIAN *keeps her eyes on the knitting pattern: on guard but not entirely frightened, aware that her mind is playing tricks on her*]

Marian You needn't try to scare me, Lily.

Lily   Don't you "Lily" me. I don't want you in here, breathing strong drink and profanity, and your husband deserted.

Marian   Maybe you'd prefer him.

Lily   I want no truck with any of you's, stay you with your own and let me rest easy with mine.

Marian   Take a look – your things are in safe hands.

Lily   The hands of an idolater!

Marian   I've changed nothing. I've brought nothing with me. See? No sacred hearts, no holy water, not even a statue of yer woman – everything still in its place the way you left it, the way you wanted it.

Lily   You're here. With all that's in you. [*Entering the kitchen*] This house was my life.

Marian   I know it was.

Lily   You know nothing about it. You'd be singing on the other side of your face if my Alfie was here.

Marian   [*Closing her eyes*] There's nobody here. Nobody.

Lily   It was Alfie Matthews found this house, it was him that first put down the deposit, moved the pair of us into it. within a week of them building it – the year of nineteen and eighteen – and me a bride at eighteen years of age . . . Alfie had come back, that's why. Back from Passchendaele. Hellfire Corner. Back from the dead. Him and Jackie Midgely, the only two from Hope Street, out of the twelve that went. All in the one week, married and moved in, he wouldn't wait . . . not after what he'd seen . . . this house was his life, same as mine. He never left it, not for a night. Except the once, to try and find work, in the Depression. That and the day they carried him to his grave. You have no right to be in here.

Marian   [*Raising the brandy*] Alfie Matthews, God rest him. [*Swigs*] No doubt he was fond of a drop himself.

Lily   My man would take a stout like any other, of a Friday night, what harm in that? He never lifted his hand to me, not once, in forty-one years of marriage, no matter what amount of drink was on him.

Marian   Must have died in '59, then.

Lily   He never harmed a living soul . . .

Marian	Fifteen years left on your own.
Lily	Every pipe in this house was laid by his hands, the plumbing, the gas, gas fitting was his trade, every pipe had to be put back and it was him put them back . . . after your crowd burnt it down round us.
Marian	I don't want to hear this.
Lily	Three years we'd been in this street.
Marian	No end to reprisals, is there . . .
Lily	Three years of sacrificing for every little stick we possessed, all that we'd managed to scrape together, destroyed in the one night, it's a mercy we even lived through it, me crouched in there, in that pantry, crying out for the Lord Jesus to deliver us, Alfie out in the yard trying to block up the back door, but they come over the wall and bate him senseless to the ground and on into this very kitchen roaring and rampaging like the cruel heathens they were, smashing through those gas mantles with their clubs and cudgels till the whole house went up. I was trapped in that pantry for a solid hour, [*She moves back towards the pantry door*] Alfie lying bleeding in the yard, if it hadn't been for the fire brigade lads moving in as fast as they did, I wouldn't be here now.
Marian	You're not here now.
Lily	Smoke and ashes, scorched walls, water flooded everywhere . . . my beautiful house . . . there was sky showing through a part of the rafters . . . every wee thing we'd saved up for ruined in the one night. By a pack of Fenian savages!
Marian	It was probably nothing personal, Lily.
Lily	Stay you away from where you're not welcome.
Marian	I have a problem with that, you see . . . seeing as the place where I'm least welcome of all is the inside of my own skull . . . so there's something we can agree on at least, Lily. I don't like me either.
	[*From offstage comes the sound of urgent hammering at the front door.* MARIAN *looks out into the hall, tense*]
Marian	Is this maybe a return bout – your mob calling round to take care of me? What do you think?
	[*She turns her head back, but* LILY *has melted away into the shadows of the pantry*]

[*The hammering is heard again*]

[MARIAN *moves out into the hall and calls*]

Marian   Who's there, please?

Ruth   [*Offstage*] It's me, Marian. It's Ruth.

Marian   Ruth, is that you? Hang on a minute.

[*She exits, and we hear her opening the front door off*]

Marian   [*Off*] Come on in, what are you doing down here at this hour?

Ruth   [*Off*] I wasn't sure of the house.

Marian   Go ahead.

[*We hear the front door being closed*]

[RUTH *appears in the kitchen doorway, dressed in a long white raincoat, with a scarf wound tightly round her neck and a bandanna on her head, worn low over the eyes*]

Ruth   None of them seem to be working, the lamps. Out there.

Marian   They've stripped all the timers out of them, for the bombs.

Ruth   Yes. They do actually do that.

Marian   How did you track me down here, Ruth?

Ruth   I'm sorry, Marian.

Marian   I was only wondering.

Ruth   I suppose your idea is to sell all these old things.

Marian   Sit down.

Ruth   Nice big fire. [*She moves to it but doesn't sit down*] It was just, earlier today, bumping into Lenny, are you really going to live down here, it's all a bit . . . all . . .

Marian   You need a drink?

Ruth   It's quite hard, getting here. That fire's quite warm.

[*She yawns*]

Marian   You might as well tell me about it, Ruth.

Ruth   I was just wondering, I know it's rather late to be asking, I would have phoned only you haven't got one, I did actually phone, at the flat, and the shop, not knowing, but anyway – if there was any chance, you could maybe put me up for the night. Marian.

Marian	What has he done to you this time?
	[RUTH *moves around, looking evasively out into the kitchen and the yard*]
Ruth	I have decided, actually. To leave – David.
Marian	Take your coat off.
Ruth	It was, rather sudden. I'll need to get, you know . . . get my things, tomorrow. It was just, tonight, I couldn't think, where else . . . he might try . . . [*Yawns*] . . . he wouldn't know . . . down here's the last place he'd think.
Marian	Just sit down. [*Guiding her into the rocking chair*] Ruth – there's blood seeping through this, I'm going to take it off . . .
Ruth	No, no, leave it, it's nothing, I just give my head a crack . . .
Marian	I'm taking it off, Ruth.
Ruth	[*Clinging to the bandanna*] . . . getting out of the car it was, just a bump, honest . . .
Marian	[*Sharply*] Let go! [*She begins to undo the bandanna*]
Ruth	Oh, no, it's not, it's not . . . oh, no, no, oh no, oh no, no no no no no . . . [*It has developed into an uncontrollable cry, her whole body rocking back and forward*] . . . oh no . . . no . . . NO!
Marian	[*As she struggles with the bandanna*] All right, Ruth. It's okay. You're all right now.
	[*She gets the bandanna off to reveal a livid, glistening, purplish-red weal slantwise across* RUTH*'s forehead, and her hair wet with blood*]
Ruth	No . . . No . . . NO!
Marian	[*Holding her hands*] It's all over. You're safe now. You're safe here. Easy, now. Hold on, Ruth. I'm just going to get something for that wound.
	[*She runs out to the bathroom*]
	[RUTH *begins to quieten*]
	[MARIAN *returns, clutching Lily Matthews' old-fashioned wooden first-aid box. She takes out lint and antiseptic and proceeds to clean* RUTH*'s wounds during the continuing dialogue*]
Marian	Okay. This should sort you out. It looks to me like Army Surplus from the Dardanelles campaign. Definitely guaranteed to separate the women from the girls. [*As she swabs the wound*] Does that hurt?

Ruth	[*Nodding*] Unh.
Mari.n	Terrific. What in God's name did he hit you with? The lawnmower or what?
Ruth	The, the . . . truncheon . . .
Marian	[*Stopping work*] His police truncheon? He took that to you?
	[RUTH *starts to sob again a little*]
Marian	All right, all right, as you were. We'll have to get this X-rayed, there could easily be concussion . . .
Ruth	There's no . . . no . . .
Marian	Is your sight blurred?
Ruth	No. Never fainted.
Marian	Well. We'll see about that in the morning. I'll put you in Lily's bed tonight, I can kip down here. It's a lot warmer anyhow.
Ruth	I'm – sorry.
Marian	Lily's our hostess here, in case you're wondering. Lily Matthews. It's her house. All her gear. I haven't touched anything, I don't want anything tidied up or touched, Ruth, that's the one stipulation I have to make, about you staying here.
Ruth	Is she not . . . dead?
Marian	She was the same age as the century. Born 1900. Married 1918. Disposessed – for the first time anyway – 1921.
Ruth	How do you know?
Marian	I've started going through her belongings. Her whole life's here, all intact. Her husband died in 1959. She changed not a single detail from then till the day she died herself, two months ago. [*Finishing her ministrations*] There. That should keep you healthy for a bit longer. How does it feel?
Ruth	Okay.
Marian	Yeah, like a bandaged migraine. Time for that drink now. [*Producing brandy*] For me, I mean. Not that you can't join me if you absolutely insist on it.
	[*She takes a swig, hands it to* RUTH *who pours a capful and drinks it from the cap*]

[*They stare into the fire for a bit*]

Ruth   Remember your flat. Magdala Street. Calling round. Always the big fire. Out would come the bottle.

Marian   Rough cider in those days, girl. [*Picking up the brandy bottle*] That's the one thing that's tangibly improved. In the intervening decade.

[*She swigs. They stare into the fire*]

Ruth   We haven't done — all that well, have we.

Marian   Speak for yourself.

Ruth   Sorry.

Marian   Joke.

[RUTH *consciously rallies herself for the next bit*]

Ruth   I know what you think of David . . .

Marian   Don't talk to me about it.

Ruth   Please, Marian.

Marian   You said you'd left him. Sound move. Stick to it. He's behind you now. Receding over the horizon. Bye-bye David. There he goes. Good riddance.

Ruth   The way you did with Lenny, I suppose.

Marian   Lenny played that godawful noise, on that trombone of his, half the night, it was enough to give you a splitting headache, certainly — however, he never actually smashed me across the skull with it.

Ruth   You can't even begin to imagine the pressure the police are under . . .

Marian   I don't want to get into it, Ruth.

Ruth   I'm not making excuses for him.

Marian   He's a policeman, who strikes his wife, about the head, with his own truncheon, there are no excuses.

Ruth   I know that.

Marian   No imaginable excuses, I'm talking fractured skulls, brain damage, haemorrhages — he could have killed you!

Ruth   He's not a bad person, Marian, honest to God, his nerves are frayed away to nothing . . .

Marian   Forget it.

Ruth   They never know the minute, he's had three good mates
                      killed in his own station, and a fourth one blinded, it's the
                      waiting around all day that gets to him, all the threats and
                      the hatred and no outlet, he comes home coiled up like a
                      spring, he's frightened of his life, it's all pent up inside him . . .
                      Christ, I'm no better, sitting at home, waiting to hear the
                      worst . . . I caught my sleeve on one of his swimming trophies
                      – Waterford crystal it was – it smashed to bits in the hearth . . .
                      I just stared down stupid at the pieces like a child who knows
                      it's in for a thumping . . . it was a sort of blinding crunch and a
                      flash of light, I was lying behind the sofa then and I could feel
                      my hair getting wet . . . twice more he hit me . . . but I had
                      my arms up by then . . . the phone started to ring, I think that
                      saved me, not that he answered it, it sort of half brought him
                      round, he just stared down at me and said, "that's you sorted
                      out", and then he threw the truncheon into a corner and went
                      into the hall for his coat and I heard the front door slamming.
                      He hadn't even had his dinner. So I got up and cleaned myself
                      off – I knew then I had to go, get away – I didn't want to be
                      there when he got back, not this time – I really knew this
                      time I couldn't live with him anymore – how can you love
                      somebody once you're actually in fear of your life of him –
                      I don't blame him, Marian, but I can't stay with him, I can't
                      stand being so scared . . . I'm sorry.

                      [MARIAN *is staring into the fire.* RUTH *pours herself another capful of*
                      brandy]

Ruth   God. Look at us. Magdala Street.

Marian   Scarcely.

Ruth   All over again. Isn't it?

Marian   Not exactly.

Ruth   All those nights, landing in on you . . . boyfriends usually, it
                      was . . .

Marian   One boyfriend, it was.

Ruth   If it wasn't the shorthand and typing course. Oh well.

Marian   He was clouting you even then, Ruth.

Ruth   It was forever me crying my eyes out anyhow.

Marian   Even as the boyfriend he was at it.

Ruth	Always some thing or another.
Marian	He started it then. He started it right at the beginning. Before the troubles were ever heard of, well before he joined the police, this has nothing to do with the police. He was handing you out a regular hiding, even then, that was what brought you crying to me, night in night out, only you never owned up to it, you covered up for the bastard till you had your first miscarriage for which he was to blame . . .
Ruth	It's not true!
Marian	The lies you've told for the sake of that sadistic pig . . .
Ruth	Who are you . . . ?
Marian	Ten years of it.
Ruth	What have you got to show?
Marian	I said I didn't want to get into it.
Ruth	He's no pig, he's a human being!
Marian	All right. Enough.
Ruth	We had fights, everybody has fights, maybe you didn't, married to that pathetic piss-artist . . .
Marian	You want to stay here?
Ruth	Lenny Harrigan was a gutless dropout fit-for-nothing from the day and hour you met him, my David's out there on those streets day and night risking his life to protect other people . . .
Marian	He's done a really impressive job for you.
Ruth	If you're so very superior, Marian, what exactly are you doing here, sitting here, in a condemned slum, at one in the morning, completely alone, sitting here staring into that fire, drinking on your own, if you know so much more, just show us what it is, the secret of your massive fucking success, because the rest of us would love to know, what it is we're doing, patronising and protecting your antiques business and your husband who abandoned his law degree and has been sponging off the state ever since and his daddy the Catholic barrister who makes a fat living out of finding loopholes in the law for Republican mass murderers to slip through, and your intellectual I.R.A. friends who're busy liberating us from our legs and our brains and our children, just tell us . . . who in hell you are . . . to sit in judgement, all the time . . .

Marian   You want to stay here?

Ruth   I'm sorry.

Marian   You still want to stay?

Ruth   I'm like . . . something wild . . .

Marian   Because ground rules are needed here. There are things to
               bear in mind here. Such as. This is the third time you've left
               David and come running to me.

Ruth   Marian, don't be angry. I'm really sorry, honest to God . . .

Marian   The previous two times you went back to him. I'm beginning
               to feel like the other woman. With all the aggravation and no
               sex.

Ruth   I won't be going back again.

Marian   Where will you live?

Ruth   I – plan to find a flat.

Marian   Tomorrow? [RUTH *hesitates*] You can't live here.

Ruth   No, of course, it was just for tonight, I couldn't think where
               else . . . I mean, if it's a problem . . .

Marian   It's a problem.[*She sustains her level stare at* RUTH, *who looks
               away*] I'm hardly going to throw you out on the street, am I.
               Tomorrow you find a flat.

Ruth   I said. Look, I could easily sleep in the front parlour, that way
               I'd be no trouble at all . . .

Marian   You're not sleeping in Lily's parlour, she has the dust sheets on
               still. You'll be in her bedroom.

Ruth   Thank you.

Marian   Concerning the other matters, Ruth – the heavy burden of my
               antiques business which you feel that you've been carrying . . .

Ruth   Please, Marian . . .

Marian   The shop has in fact been taken over by Tom Feeney, the
               gallery owner, who has impeccably Protestant credentials as
               of course you well know. Lenny, just for the record, hasn't
               actually had to draw the dole since receiving an annuity from
               the same maiden aunt who left him this house in her will, the
               two friends I had who joined the Republican movement are
               no longer friends, on account of one being dead and the other

being a pious fool who's now in Long Kesh and deserves to stay there, Lenny isn't entirely my husband since we're half-way through a divorce, and I can hardly be held responsible for his da who, amongst other things, was always avid to achieve purchase on my inner thigh over the Christmas period . . .

Ruth   I remember.

Marian   Generally speaking, Ruth, in regard to these ground rules, whereas you may be a girlhood friend, you're nobody's probation officer, and if I choose to drink brandy in front of a fire in a house eloquent with the history of this city at a time of the night when I feel most sensate, that's a choice I'm making out of my own free will under my own control for my own pleasure which is a private decision not subject to invasion by anyone whatsoever . . .

[*The sound of someone opening and coming through the front door is heard from offstage*]

Ruth   Oh my God!

Marian   [*Leaping up*] Quiet!

[*She grabs a poker from the fireplace and positions herself by the kitchen door, on the non-opening side*]

[*The door is flung open – concealing* MARIAN *from view altogether – and* LENNY *enters, precipitously, since he is carrying two bulging holdalls and has his trombone case under one arm*]

Lenny   Ruth? – how did you get here? What happened to your head?

[MARIAN *reveals herself by pushing the door shut.* LENNY *registers the poker*]

Have you two been fighting each other?

Marian   What's this all about?

Lenny   Who did you imagine I was?

Marian   What are these bags?

Lenny   I've been totally burgled. The entire place, stripped clean. I was out playing at a gig. My house is like a bomb site. Well – nearly.

Marian   You're not planning on staying here?

Lenny   It's really very kind of you to sympathise, Marian – but I expect I'll get over it in time.

Ruth   Did you notify the police?

Lenny   Usual formalities. They are a bit otherwise engaged – hardly news to you.

Marian   Ruth's already staying tonight.

Lenny   Fine. Lovely. A few more arrivals and we can throw a party.

Marian   There's nowhere for you to sleep.

Lenny   Marian – I could begin to feel a trifle testy at your demeanour.

Ruth   I'll make us some tea. [*She hurries out of the hostilities into the scullery, and proceeds to put the kettle on*]

Lenny   I get home after midnight to find that everything of value I possess has been stolen, right down to the brass bed, which is particularly inconvenient since I normally use it for sleeping on . . .

Marian   There's plenty of beds in your parents' house.

Lenny   What the hell do you think you're doing here anyway?

Marian   Looking for a quiet life, quaint as that may sound to you.

Lenny   Who said you could move in, the house doesn't belong to you, not yet.

Marian   We've exchanged contracts.

Lenny   We haven't completed!

Marian   Don't start on the legalese, we've both agreed I'm buying the house, so I'm living here now and I don't want you poking your head round the door any time the fancy takes you.

Lenny   What do you imagine this is, some clever ploy to worm my way back in beneath your panty-hose, forget it – not interested.

Marian   Not on offer if you were.

Lenny   Good, that's a relief. So. You and your friend want to camp out overnight in my house, is that it?

Marian   Fuck off.

Lenny   Well, you're most welcome to, yes, certainly. First up makes breakfast. [*Calling through the door*] Find everything you need there, Ruth?

Ruth   Thanks, Lenny, yes.

Lenny	Great stuff. [*Sotto voce to* MARIAN] What's Desdemona doing here exactly?
Marian	Another refugee.
Lenny	Did he give her that head?
Marian	She's left him.
Lenny	Not again. He'll be the next one through the door, then. Just like old times, really.
Marian	Not in any respect whatsoever.
Lenny	Where's she sleeping?
Marian	Lily's bed.
Lenny	You?
Marian	In front of this fire.
Lenny	The top bedroom for me then.
Marian	The bedding's damp.
Lenny	[*Picking up one of the holdalls*] Sleeping bag.
Marian	Thoughtful of the burglars to leave you that.
Lenny	It's yours, actually. It was under the stairs.
Marian	Great. I can use it for in here. [*Takes the holdall, unzips it, removes the sleeping bag*]
Lenny	Just bear in mind, Marian – I can have you evicted from this house. If I had a mind to do it, I could still call off the sale.
Marian	I've moved in. I'm here to stay. Try it.
Lenny	You know – I was left in bits after you walked out on me. Except for enormous relief about one thing. Which I've never stopped thanking God for. I didn't have to attempt to understand you any more.
Marian	Well, I'm run ragged, Lenny. From understanding you through and through.
Ruth	[*Calling through to them*] Tea's nearly ready!
Lenny	Scrub it, Ruth. I think you'll find the milk's all curdled.
	[*He picks up his luggage and exits upstairs*]
Ruth	Will I use these mugs?

Marian   No. Leave them.

Ruth   Where are the cups?

Marian   I don't want any tea. You can use the kettle for a hot water
                   bottle. You're going to need one, in that bedroom.

Ruth   Right-o.

                   [*She looks around the scullery for it, then returns to the kitchen
                   door in a helpless kind of way*]

Marian   It's on the back of the door.

                   [RUTH *mutely fetches it*]

                   [MARIAN *has sat down again in the rocking chair and is staring into
                   the fire. From upstairs, the sound of* LENNY *playing his trombone
                   starts up: loud and up-tempo. She looks slowly up at the ceiling, at
                   the sound*]

                   [*The lights fade to blackout*]

                   [*End of Scene Two*]

III

[The night of Sunday, May 19th]

[The kitchen and scullery are dark and deserted]

*[The sound of half a dozen drunken youths running up the back entry, shouting and whistling, is heard from off. A beer bottle sails over the yard wall and smashes harmlessly on the floor of the yard. Then silence returns. Until the front door can be heard opening and two slightly drunk men (*LENNY *and* PETER*) coming into the hall]*

Lenny   *[Offstage]* Easy on.

Peter   *[Offstage]* Bloody blind man's buff . . .

Lenny   Sshh . . . *[Calling out]* Fear not, ladies, it's reinforcements. You can put the poker away!

[Sound of PETER *laughing and then stumbling]*

Lenny   Watch the bottles, for God's sake . . .

Peter   Well, get some lights on . . .

[The kitchen door is thrust open, to reveal LENNY *carrying a cardboard box full of beer cans, and bottles of spirits. He gropes round for the light switch with his free hand, makes contact, and the electric light comes on]*

Lenny   What do you know, we're in luck, head. Double luck. The electricity is on and the housemother is absent. We've got power without responsibility.

*[*PETER *has followed him into the room, carrying a travel bag and a bulky paper sack, like a small bag of cement. His style is 1974 casual chic]*

Peter   My drinking arm's gone dead with the weight of this stuff.

[He dumps the heavy sack down along with his travel bag]

Lenny   What did you have to hump that muck across the water for anyhow?

Peter   It's muesli. Grain and nuts, honey, dried fruit . . .

Lenny   It has been heard of here, you know, you don't actually have to define it.

Peter   Didn't want to use up your food supplies.

Lenny   You've brought about three stone of it.

Peter   It's very nutritious, I figured I could live on it, if the strike goes on indefinitely, do you think it might?

Lenny   You need milk.

Peter   This is true.

Lenny   You can't eat it without milk. Is what I'm saying.

Peter   Ah, holy God, they haven't stopped the milk, have they.

Lenny   Peter, use the loaf – protest strike by loyalist workers, right? Electricity cuts. No petrol supplies. No animal foodstuffs. Barricades all over the city turning back the traffic. Three quarters of all cows are Protestant. What chance has the milk got?

Peter   [*Who has been holding out his right arm, wincing*] Pins and needles.

             [LENNY *opens a can of beer from the box*]

Lenny   Here. Try it left-handed. As they say in the Marriage Guidance Council.

Peter   Do they?

Lenny   More or less.

Peter   Well, you should know. Cheers.

Lenny   And welcome home to you, old fruit.

             [*They drink*]

Peter   Do I sound very English?

Lenny   Yeah, but only when you talk.

Peter   Don't you just love it – the sly dig, the dry remark, how painfully I've missed it. The authentic Lilliputian wit. [*Moving round, surveying the rooms*] And this is the inheritance?

Lenny   It's the best I can do for you tonight.

Peter   An ethnic little gem, though. What? Set this load down in a choicer part of Birmingham, a treasure trove is what you'd have, my son, a highly des. res. in need of minor gentrification.

Lenny   You're welcome to ship the whole lot back with you, I can't believe you managed to get over here. Or why.

Peter   I did have to hang about most of the night, it's true – waiting for the blasted ferry to make up its mind to sail from Heysham.

Lenny	There can only have been you on it.
Peter	Well, aside from a coach party of foreign travel agents, and a young soldier's wife.
Lenny	No doubt you took care of her.
Peter	Once she got her horrible kids to sleep. It was the travel agents who were really in need of looking after, though. Wholesale shitlessness.
Lenny	How did you get the booze?
Peter	Bribed the barman.
Lenny	Jesus. See you, head? People like you lead a charmed life. If I hadn't just chanced to sneak across town this evening . . . you do realise it's mob law here at the minute?
Peter	I've been watching it all week. The BBC have adapted it for television, you know.
Lenny	I haven't been living in my own place for nearly a month, since the burglary, I hadn't even set foot in it in the last four days, since the strike got heavy – it was a pure fluke, showing up there tonight, just in time to bump into you. Anybody but you could have been in a tightish corner.
Peter	I placed my faith in the Ulster Sunday. I believed in my heart, brother – even if the Protestant blackshirts had finally staged a putsch, they would still remember the seventh day and keep it holy. Not to mention rainy, bleak, doom-laden, and utterly devoid of human life. Sure enough. I was able to roam at will around the mean streets – apart from the occasional catcall, and comment of a personal nature.
Lenny	You didn't want to miss all the stir, I suppose.
Peter	It sounds to me like the big picture. The '74 Uprising. The Great Loyalist Insurrection. Historic days in Lilliput.
Lenny	Sure, every bloody day in the week's historic, in this place.
Peter	Anyway, I was due a trip home. It's been three years.
Lenny	You're not going to go on calling it Lilliput the whole time?
Peter	What, this teeny weeny wee province of ours and its little people, all the angry munchkins, with their midget brains, this festering pimple on the vast white flabby bum of western Europe, what would _you_ call it?

Lenny   I call it home.

Peter   You do realise – the rest of the world has crossed the street,
              long since, passed on by – on account of having fully-grown
              twentieth-century problems to be getting on with – the
              continued existence of the planet, say, or the survival of the
              species?

Lenny   So is that what they fight about in Birmingham?

Peter   What am I hearing? For God's sake don't tell me you've turned
              into a proud wee Ulsterman?

Lenny   Coals to Newcastle, okay? Coals of fire, in this case, you get
              them heaped on your head here every time you turn round.
              The last thing I need is you landing in and dumping another
              load on me.

Peter   Only the truth. Crass insensitivity. Craven apologies. Not
              another slur against the dear wee darling homeland shall pass
              these lips.

Lenny   It's the arsehole of hell, who's arguing. No future in it.
              Whatsoever. Once this Prod agitation is over, I'm off out, I've
              definitely had enough, I know what you're going to say.

Peter   All right – but apart from that . . .

Lenny   What? Apart from what?

Peter   Apart from the fact that you've said it all a dozen times
              before . . .

Lenny   Dammit, Peter, I knew that's what you were going to say!

Peter   I wasn't going to say it, you asked me to say it.

Lenny   I'm serious. I mean it.

Peter   All right.

Lenny   Things have changed. Is what I'm saying.

Peter   All right. Always assuming it ever will be over, of course.

Lenny   What? The strike? 'Course it will.

Peter   Strike? This is no strike. [*Paisleyite voice*] This is a
              constitutional stoppage!

Lenny   God save us, Doctor, that sounds agonising, is there nothing
              you could prescribe that would shift it?

Peter	I mean, what if they do take over, for keeps? They'll throw all you Fenian rebels into the Gulag – make you earn your supplementary benefit sewing mailbags.
Lenny	What makes you think you'd be let off?
Peter	Me, I'm one of the elect – my daddy's even a minister of the true faith.
Lenny	You're joking, he's a Methodist. Out on the barricades there, that counts as dangerous left-wing subversion. Your da's ecumenical!
Peter	All right, keep your voice down.
Lenny	Anyhow, with that hair and those jeans, and the way you talk – not to mention the muesli –
Peter	All right, all right, I've got the gag.
Lenny	Never you fret, head, it'll be over within the week.
Peter	Somebody on the boat was saying they'd declared a state of emergency.
Lenny	Meaning the army's finally going to be ordered to break it. The English have just been hanging on as usual, waiting for reason and moderation and fair play to break out suddenly – you know – just like it always does in the Houses of Parliament.
Peter	[*Parliamentary braying*] Heah heah, heah heah heah . . .
Lenny	[*Joining in*] Heah heah heah . . . [*Laughs*] . . . yeah, right. So anyhow. You still like it over there?
Peter	It's a lot bigger.
Lenny	Well. This is it. [*A gap has opened in the banter*]
Peter	And how about you? You're actually going to attempt the great escape this time?
Lenny	Nothing to keep me here now. Apart from three hundred-odd street barricades, and thousands of hooded men with clubs.
	[*The front door being opened is heard from off*]
Peter	Is that Marian?
Lenny	Look, just remember what I told you, right?
Peter	I'm cool.

Lenny	Leave her to me.
Peter	All yours.

[*They are all tensed up in anticipation of the onslaught*]

[*The door from the hall opens, and* RUTH *enters, carrying a heavy bale of peat briquettes in one hand, and a Bible in the other. She is dressed in her Sunday best*]

Ruth	Sorry . . .
Lenny	Ah, Ruth. It's you.
Ruth	Look what Marian's mother gave us. For the fire.
Lenny	Did Marian come back with you?
Ruth	She's just parking her car. Up behind our church. There's a car park there.
Lenny	Good thinking.
Ruth	It's a bit safer.
Peter	I'm glad to hear those old buildings are being put to some practical use.
Ruth	It's the Church of God, it was only built last year.
Lenny	By the way, Ruth, this here is a friend of mine from student days, Peter Irwin. [*To the latter*] This is Ruth Macalester.
Ruth	[*As she sets the bale of peat down in the hearth*] How'd you do.
Peter	Fancy a beer?
Ruth	I have to change, excuse me.

[*She exits, up the stairs*]

Peter	Protestant nookie, in the house, why wasn't I informed.
Lenny	She was supposed to be moving to her ma's this morning.
Peter	Not a bad arse on her.
Lenny	Forget it, she's one of Marian's lame ducks.
Peter	Not the cop's wife again?
Lenny	She left him three weeks ago, serious GBH. She's been holed up here ever since.
Peter	My God, so you've been besieged, all this time, with not just one but two frigid cows – lucky I turned up, head. You're in serious need of reinforcements.

Lenny	Listen. Go easy with Marian.
Peter	What? I haven't even clapped eyes on her yet.
Lenny	I know how to handle her, it's just, when she sees you here – she's definitely going to cut up rough.
Peter	Sure. Yeah. Marian and me were never exactly a mutual admiration society.
Lenny	It's not that, it's the state she's in . . . totally obsessive, don't ask me what the story is . . . some weird syndrome, you know how it is with women. I'm just thankful she's finally agreed to a divorce.
Peter	Would it still be losing the kid, maybe?
Lenny	That? – oh, she took that in her stride . . . didn't she . . . no problem. Anyhow. It's five years now.
Peter	Can't be.
Lenny	Near as dammit. August '69.
Peter	A vintage month.
Lenny	The marriage started to go dead too, from then on.
Peter	Bound to. The pair of you had never intended to hitch up in the first place. Not until the pregnancy.
Lenny	Yeah, but let me tell you a funny story. When the sprog was born – Christopher, to give him his due and proper name – the bunched-up fingers and feet, like tight fat buds, flailing away at us . . . when he was there between us on the bed, all crinkled-up and livid . . . something out of order happened. Between Marian and me. We sort of fell in love. With each other. At least I know I did, she would sneer at all that now, don't ever let me catch you breathing a word of this . . .
Peter	Swear.
Lenny	. . . I'd stake my life on it, if you really want to know, so there we were. Married lovers, the way it's always supposed to be in the booklets. It wasn't exactly a pleasure trip, there was very little sleep, money was tight, we didn't get out a lot. It's the one time so far I've ever felt one hundred per cent alive. For five months. That was how long it lasted . . . that was how long the sprog lasted. At that point he checked out, he'd seen enough. Maybe it was the prospect of having me as a da, you could hardly blame him . . . she came down in the morning . . . the cot was still, no more fury . . . just a tiny silent shrivelled-

up rickle of bones and skin. She came and woke me. She took it in her stride. I picked him up . . . you didn't know this. Any of it. He was my son. She was my wife.

[PETER *is left at a loss for a few moments. Then he fetches a can of beer from the box, opens it and offers it to* LENNY. LENNY *takes it and drinks deep*]

[*The sound of somebody coming in from the street is heard from off. After a moment,* MARIAN *enters from the hall, in church-going clothes also, carrying a bag of dry foods*]

Marian	My God.
Peter	Hello there, Marian.
Marian	The lulu's back in town. How did you get here?
Peter	Oh, you know – the spirit moved me.
Marian	So how long has the spirit dumped you here for?
Peter	That's really up to the Ulster Workers' Council.
Marian	Hang on a minute. You went off and qualified as a property surveyor. Is that right?
Peter	It's what pays the rent.
Marian	I imagine it does. You need a place to stay?
Lenny	In actual point of fact . . .
Marian	Here's an offer. You can have the boxroom upstairs for a week. In return for doing me a professional full-scale written structural survey of the house.
Peter	What for?
Marian	What do you say?
Peter	If you like.
Marian	I've got some people coming from the National Trust on Thursday, that's when you have to do it by. Deal?
Peter	Fine.
Marian	Very good, Peter, glad you managed back.

[*She moves on into the kitchen to unload her bag*]

Lenny	Hold it just a minute. What has the National Trust got to do with anything?
Marian	Very little, in your case.

Peter	[*To* MARIAN] Is the survey meant to be shown to them or something?
Marian	Given to then.
Peter	Why on earth?
Marian	Because I'm making them an offer too. To take over this house as a National Trust property.
Lenny	Take over – here? This?

[*It's too much for him, he lets out a bellow of incredulous laughter*]

[*Peter grimaces at him to be quiet and moves to the kitchen door*]

Peter	[*To* MARIAN] Is it really – their style, though? Marian? Would you say? The National Trust?
Marian	Not yet, it isn't.
Peter	I mean, it certainly does have plenty of atmosphere . . .
Lenny	God knows, fish could nearly swim in it.
Peter	It's just, you know – all those Castle Coole and Castleward types of places . . .
Lenny	It's all those fully upholstered la-di-da lady baritones, Jesus wept, can you imagine them in here, selling postcards of the outside bog and knitted tea cosies?
Marian	I'm glad I'm keeping you entertained.
Peter	Where on earth did you get the idea, Marian?
Marian	Lily Matthews lived here. 1900 to 1974. This house was her whole life. She never threw anything away. I've started cataloguing it all. Every last thimble and shirt stud, every grocery bill and cigarette card and rationing coupon, every document of her and Alfie's life together.

[*She scoops up some documents from a shoe box on the sideboard*]

Look at this – the dismissal from his gasfitting job in 1931. They were able to manage through the Depression by finding a lodger to take in – that's his rent book there. Alan Ferris. He was an English airman. His photograph's here. The three of them together.

[*She carefully scrutinises the photograph*]

Peter	Right. Yeah. Though, there must be thousands of houses like this . . . thousands of people, like that. It's very touching, absolutely – but it's nothing special, though. Is it?

Marian   You think not? So why should Lily Matthews' home and
                hearth be less special than Lord Castlereagh's or the Earl
                of Enniskillen's? A whole way of life, a whole culture,
                the only difference being, that this home speaks for a far
                greater community of experience in this country than some
                transplanted feeble-minded aristocrat's ever could, have you
                looked at it, properly?

Peter   Haven't had a chance yet.

Marian   Never mind what you learnt as a student architect, this is what
                design and building and history mean, to the people of this
                city, go ahead. Look around it. Just don't touch anything, I've
                changed nothing. Lenny, show him where the boxroom is.

Lenny   Why can't he sleep in the front parlour?

Marian   It's a front parlour, that's why.

Lenny   Exactly. Instead of being a boxroom.

Peter   Why don't I just take my gear upstairs, while I'm at it. [*Picking
                up his travel bag and making an exit out the hall door and up the
                stairs*]

Lenny   [*To* MARIAN] The National Trust . . . you're not actually serious?

Marian   No more refugees. There are three too many as it is.

Lenny   [*Gesturing towards the bag*] Help yourself to the muesli.

                [*He exits in pursuit of* PETER]

                [MARIAN *closes the door behind them. She crosses to the rocking
                chair, sits down in it, and stares into the empty grate*]

                [*From the far distance, the sound of two lambeg drums head-to-
                head starts up*]

                [LILY MATTHEWS *appears from the pantry. She comes right into the
                kitchen, to behind the rocking chair. She looks to be in late middle
                age now, but wearing a pretty print dress from the early thirties
                with a pinafore over it, and her hair drawn up in a bun*]

Lily   You needn't bother getting settled. You'll have no peace in
                this house, nor good fortune neither.

Marian   What kind of fortune did you have, Lily?

Lily   Four of you's now, in on me, tramping your filth all over my
                good floors.

Marian   We'll have it back to ourselves, you and me, soon enough.
                Back to rights.

Lily	You've been to your Mass again, I can smell it off you.
Marian	Something I've been meaning to ask you . . .
Lily	Why did you come here? What possessed you to move in on me?
Marian	Fifteen years, all on your own. The neighbours leaving one by one, blind houses blocked up behind them, the street gradually silenced. Shut up in here. The loneliness of it.
Lily	I had my own people round me, never wanted for anything.
Marian	I've been lonely myself, you see.
Lily	Never wanted company . . .
Marian	Five years now.
Lily	Quite content on my own, thank you.
Marian	That's why.
Lily	Up until you turned up. Four of you's now, in on me.
Marian	Company like that only makes you lonelier, you think I don't understand that, you think I want them here either?
Lily	Don't you imagine you can find favour with me, dear, when you couldn't even make a decent life with your own husband, your own sort.
Marian	That's the dress you were wearing in that photograph.
Lily	Stay you out of my private belongings!
Marian	In the name of Jesus I'm trying to preserve them!
Lily	Don't you dare blaspheme in my kitchen!
Marian	Sorry, I'm sorry . . .
Lily	Nobody asked your help and it's not wanted.
Marian	It's not help that I'm offering . . . it's help that I'm looking for. Is that not obvious?
	[LILY *begins to sing*]
Lily	Oh, God our help in ages past . . .
Marian	Don't fight me, Lily , . . .
Lily	[*Continuing to sing over* MARIAN's *lines*] Our hope for years to come . . .
Marian	I need you, we have got to make this work, you and me . . .

Lily   [*Singing on regardless*]
              Our shelter from the stormy blast,
              And our eternal home!

Marian   You think you're haunting me, don't you. But you see it's me
              that's actually haunting you. I'm not going to go away. There's
              no curse or hymn that can exorcise me. So you might as well
              just give me your blessing and make your peace with me, Lily.

Lily   You'll have no peace in this house.

Marian   Why had you no wee'uns? You weren't able, was that it?

Lily   Never had a day's sickness in my life, there was nothing the
              matter with me or mine.

Marian   So it was Alfie, then?

Lily   That's no business of yours or of your like, my Alfie was a good
              man, he would have made a loving father, if the Good Lord
              didn't see fit to send us a little one, so be it, he giveth and
              he taketh away, blessed be the name of the Lord. Anyway, I
              haven't noticed you bringing up any youngsters.

Marian   No. The Lord didn't do too well by me either. In that respect.

Lily   What right does a hussy like you have, to question God's will?
              Why would he bless the fruit of your womb more than or
              mine, look at this place, you have it like a pigsty . . . are there
              not enough runty litters running the streets, whelped by your
              kind, reared with a half-brick in their fists, and the backsides
              hanging out of their trousers?

              [MARIAN *has reached into the raffia basket tucked in by the side of
              the rocking chair*]

Marian   It was just that I found this.

              [*She takes out and holds up a 1930's child's christening gown,
              trimmed with lace and ribbons*]

Lily   [*Terrified*] The devil . . .

Marian   Folded up.

Lily   The devil is in this house . . .

Marian   Wrapped in tissue.

Lily   The Antichrist is in our midst!

Marian   Hidden amongst your underwear.

              [LILY *backs away into the scullery*]

Lily   Oh, Lord Jesus, send the devil out of this room, let your
                servant now depart in peace . . . [*She is melting into the shadows
                once again*]

                [RUTH *comes in from the hall*]

Ruth   Is he away?

Marian   What? Who?

Ruth   The friend of Lenny's. Peter.

Marian   He's staying here.

Ruth   [*Seeing the christening robe*] Och, look, isn't that the loveliest
                thing . . . was it hers? I thought there were no children?

Marian   Maybe she lived in hope. Like you and me.

Ruth   Not me, Marian. Not now.

Marian   You're not even thirty. There's a whole life to come.

Ruth   They don't think . . . after I lost the third one . . . they told me
                that . . . it mightn't . . .

Marian   It's a childless house. Barren. Why else would I feel so much
                at home.

Ruth   What do you know about it, yours was alive, at least you had
                it at your breast, for a while at least, you knew what it was, oh
                Jesus if only I'd been able to keep just one of them, to hold it
                back to make it grow, we'd be all right, all different, if I can't
                have a child I won't live!

Marian   Christopher would have been five in August. Starting school.
                If he hadn't gone. Left me. Given up the ghost in me. My own
                soul, left for dead. He was our future, you see. Future, at a
                time like this . . . what could it possibly mean – a future? In a
                place like this?

                [*She looks down at* LILY'*s unused Christening robe.* RUTH *goes to her,
                kneels by her, embraces her*]

                [*The light fades to blackout, on the grief of the three women*]

                [*End of Scene Three*]

Act 2

IV

[*The night of Saturday, May 25th*]

[*The house is in darkness*]

[*Over the theatre P.A., we hear the opening of a broadcast to the nation being given by the Prime Minister, Harold Wilson*]

Broadcast Tape
As this holiday weekend begins, Northern Ireland faces the gravest crisis in her history. It is a crisis equally for all of us who live on this side of the water. What we are seeing in Northern Ireland is not just an industrial strike. It has nothing to do with wages. It has nothing to do with jobs – except to imperil jobs. It is a deliberate and calculated attempt to use every undemocratic and unparliamentary means for the purpose of bringing down the whole constitution of Northern Ireland so as to set up there a sectarian and undemocratic state . . .

[RUTH *has come into the kitchen from the hall, with a lighted candle in one hand and a transistor radio in the other. The sound of the broadcast from her radio overlaps with and soon takes over from the theatre P.A*]

Radio
. . . We recognise that behind this situation lie many genuine and deeply held fears. I have to say that these fears are unfounded. That they are being deliberately fostered by people in search of power.

[PETER *has followed* RUTH *into the kitchen, carrying a lighted oil lamp. She has set her candle down on the mantelpiece and the radio on the table, and has sat down to listen. He places the oil lamp on the sideboard, and also sits down to listen*]

Radio
The people on this side of the water – British parents – have seen their sons vilified and spat upon and murdered. British taxpayers have seen the taxes they have poured out, almost without regard to cost – over three hundred million pounds a year this year with the cost of the Army operation on top of that – going into Northern Ireland. They see property destroyed by evil violence and are asked to pick up the bill for rebuilding it. Yet people who benefit from all this now

viciously defy Westminster, purporting to act as though they were an elected government; people who spend their lives sponging on Westminster and British democracy and then systematically assault democratic methods. Who do these people think they are?

[RUTH *springs up in a fury and switches the radio off*]

Peter	Hey.
Ruth	How dare he?
Peter	He hasn't finished.
Ruth	How dare he say that to us? – <u>us</u> – spongers!
Peter	What's the odds?
Ruth	We worked hard for everything we have and hold, we're British taxpayers just the same as they are!
Peter	He's talking about the seizing of power!
Ruth	This city was full of life, full of industry, built by our people, they made it into a capital city, to be proud of . . .
Peter	All right.
Ruth	Everything we have and hold, for five long years now we've watched it rent asunder, pulverised into rubble by the real spongers, cruel and murderous bastards . . .
Peter	All right!
Ruth	How long are we supposed to grin and bear it?
Peter	I haven't noticed much grinning.
Ruth	We've had enough, far more than enough.
Peter	So this is your idea of a solution?
Ruth	Something had to be done!
Peter	No food, no light, no heat, the bullet-heads in charge?
Ruth	That smug wee English shite with his weaselly voice, what right has he to lecture us, he'll soon know his driver, the same boyo . . .
Peter	He isn't here, Ruthie child, he's five hundred-odd miles in that direction, over the sea, fully fed and comfortable, this is being done to us, the people here, self-inflicted, is this what you want? – the apemen in charge, shops without

food to sell, garages without petrol, people penned into their own homes, cold hungry and terrified, there's a mile-long queue of doctors and nurses and social workers, and lawyers, up at Hawthornden Road, queuing up to beg for a special pass to get them through the barricades to their patients and clients, and from who? – from the wee hard men who can barely sign their name to their special bloody passes, from shipyard Bible-thumpers, unemployed binmen, petty crooks and extortionists, pigbrain mobsters and thugs, they've seized control over all of us, they're now ordering the sewage workers out, the raw sewage is about to come flooding down those streets out there, and it won't be the English who die of typhoid, Ruth, this is not what we call a protest movement, this is what is historically known as root and branch fascism . . .

Ruth   Just shut up and listen for a minute!

Peter   We're at the mercy of actual real-life fascist jackboot rule!

Ruth   Use your ears, just listen. Out there. Right? Nothing. No gunplay. No bombs. How long is it – how long, since you could go to sleep at night, without that? Of course you wouldn't know, would you.

Peter   What does that prove?

Ruth   The I.R.A. have been stopped in their tracks at last.

Peter   For Christ's sake, they're on hold, that's all, you're doing it all for them, alienate the Brits, that broadcast was like music to their ears, are you deaf, blind and entirely thick?

Ruth   Don't you condescend to me . . .

Peter   Can you not see, this whole tribe, so-called Protestants, we both of us grew up in it, all that endless mindless marching, they've been marching away with the lambegs blattering and the banners flying straight up a dead-end one-way blind alley, self-destroying, the head's eating the tail now, it's a lingering tribal suicide going on out there, there was no need for any of it, they held all the cards, they only needed to be marginally generous, how did I get into this, I apologise for what I called you, I got carried away, fear no doubt, funny isn't it . . . it's not as if I'm unfamiliar with tense situations. Six years ago, I was standing in a human chain encircling a building. It was in America . . . a university. Black students had seized the building and smuggled in guns, the police were lined up in their hundreds, ready to storm it. Me and a fewscore of other white liberals had put our bodies in between, holding hands with each other, armed blacks behind us and armed cops in front . . . it was scary as hell, but there was playacting involved too, a big American psychodrama, the college president and the blacks' leader were up on a stage together at the end, hugging each other, I don't quite see that happening here. God, I'm hungry. Do you want some muesli?

[*He goes to the sack and spoons some into a bowl*]

Ruth   You don't know what's been happening here. What the people have gone through. How could you. You got out.

Peter   Why are the police not intervening, this is wholesale lawlessness . . . why are the Army standing aside, watching people being roughed up, vehicles being hijacked, shops being looted, doing sod-all about it? Who's supposed to be in charge?

Ruth   They can't take on an entire community. You don't know your own people, not any more. This strike is theirs. They're completely behind it now. Nationalist rebels have been imposed as executive ministers, ruling over them, against their will . . .

Peter   Do us a favour . . .

Ruth   They won't be coerced. They won't be dictated to. All they're proving is what your sort was always chanting – the power lies with the people. Only in this case it's your own people. You have no notion how they feel, you opted out. You lost touch. You see it all like the English now, "a plague on both their houses" . . . easy to say when it isn't your own house that's in mortal danger.

Peter   I haven't exactly noticed you manning the barricades.

Ruth   There's no shortage of volunteers.

Peter   And this is what your husband makes of it all?

Ruth   My husband and I are separated.

Peter   He hasn't tracked you down yet, then?

Ruth   I wrote. Told him – not to bother.

[*She bites her lip, fighting back the tears*]

Peter   That's the stuff. [*Proffering the bowl of muesli*] Have some of this.

Ruth   No thanks.

Peter   [*Pouring milk on the muesli*] Just the powdered milk, I'm afraid.
            Go ahead. [*She shakes her head*] Sure? [*He shovels a spoonful
            into his mouth, munches it*] It's not bad at all, actually. [*He takes
            another spoonful*] Aaggh! [*He clutches his jaw in pain, thrusting
            the muesli bowl aside*]

Ruth   What's up?

Peter   Bugger it.

Ruth   Broken filling?

Peter   All I need.

Ruth   It's those wee black things. [*Looking in the bowl*] Lenny says it's
            buckshot.

Peter   They're seeds.

Ruth   Do you want an aspirin? He says he read it on the
            packaging . . .

Peter   Buckwheat!

Ruth   How did you find such a big bag of that stuff?

Peter   American couple, downstairs. Made it up for me.

Ruth   You mean in Birmingham?

Peter   They have a health-food shop. Under my flat.

Ruth   It's tasteless muck, isn't it.

Peter   Well, it hasn't been fried sodden, in rancid lard, if that's what
            you mean. So it scarcely counts as fit to eat at all, in this wee
            province of ours.

Ruth   You don't think very much of us, do you.

Peter   Why can I never remember it, until the minute I set foot
            . . . that ache in the arse, whatever the direct opposite of
            homesickness is. Exilephilia. The desperate nagging pain of
            longing to be far, far away.

Ruth   In Birmingham, you mean? Do you really like it there?

Peter   It's a lot bigger.

Ruth   It's where all the roads are, isn't it.

            [*She goes into the kitchen and fetches him a glass of water and two
            aspirin*]

Here. Take these.

Peter [*Taking the glass*] What are we supposed to do when they turn this stuff off?

Ruth I've already filled up every receptacle in the house.

Peter Amazing . . .

Ruth We'll get by fine. Sooner or later the English will cave in, they have to. They'll disband the executive.

Peter Out of the whole four of us – you're the only one who's really coping with all this.

Ruth I just like having things to do. Looking after people. At school I always wanted to be a nurse, really bad . . .

Peter The uniform would suit you.

Ruth Only trouble being, it's the sort of thing you need a good stomach for.

Peter Looks terrific from here.

Ruth No, I mean, you know what I mean, not the uniform. Blood and things. Not my strong point. I've always been quite well organised, though.

Peter Lucky somebody is, in this house.

Ruth Is it really bad? The tooth?

Peter A slight throb, that's all. Sorry I blew a fuse earlier.

Ruth Don't mention it.

Peter Kiss and make up, then.

Ruth That's right.

Peter I've been meaning to ask you, how did you and Marian come to be friends?

Ruth The swimming.

Peter What swimming?

Ruth We both swam for our schools, we got selected for the Northern Ireland youth squad. We went away to Scotland and Holland. She was nearly seventeen, I was only thirteen, I wasn't like you, I was desperately homesick, it used to be the buses and trams that set me off the worst – the funny colour of them, I cried my eyes out over that. Honest to God, the things you feel. I'm no different, even now. Anyhow. It was Marian looked after me, she was like a big sister. We just somehow stayed friends, from that day to this.

Peter   It must be the swimming that keeps your figure so lithe.

Ruth   Oh, I don't compete now . . . not since my marriage . . . just for the club occasionally . . . you see, David, my husband, he was a real championship swimmer, I met him then too.

Peter   Lucky fellow.

Ruth   Not in his book.

Peter   You must have been spoilt for choice, with your looks.

Ruth   Oh, yes. Fighting them off.

Peter   Bet you were.

Ruth   Some hope.

Peter   You're quite remarkable, Ruth. In my book, that is.

Ruth   Not me.

Peter   Can I ask you something?

Ruth   Up to you.

Peter   It may seem a bit presumptuous.

Ruth   What is it?

Peter   Supposing we really were to kiss and make up?

Ruth   What sort of a question's that . . .

[*He's kissing her. Slowly and tentatively, she begins to respond*]

[*He guides her to the sofa, sits her down, lifts her legs on to the sofa so that she is lying with her knees bent, and him kneeling by her. He kisses her again, gently nudging her skirt up over her knees, and caressing her thighs*]

[*The sound of Lenny's solo trombone suddenly blares out from upstairs.* RUTH *thrusts* PETER *aside and sits up*]

Ruth   What's he doing here?

Peter   They were both supposed to be searching for the car.

Ruth   He must have been dossing up there this whole time, he could easy have been in on us!

[*She is hurriedly pulling down her skirt and sitting up straight*]

Peter	Easy, it's all right, we'll go into the front parlour.
Ruth	We can't do that, not in there.
Peter	There's a lock on the door.
Ruth	Lily always kept it special!
Peter	It's a room, that's all. It's privacy.
Ruth	Marian would kill me!
Peter	Ruth, it's our business. It's strictly between us. Our secret. You and me.

[*Strokes her hair, gently kisses her again. Then he takes the candle and leads her by the hand, out the hall door and towards the forbidden pleasures of the front parlour*]

[*Lenny's trombone continues for a while from upstairs*]

[*There is a sudden hammering from outside the backyard door.* MARIAN's *voice is heard shouting "Lenny! Lenny! Hello! Down here! Open up!"*]

[*The trombone music stops and* LENNY *is heard thundering down the stairs: he appears rushing in from the hall carrying a torch, and continues straight through the kitchen to the scullery door, which he unlocks and opens; and thence down the yard to the yard door which he unbolts and flings back – to reveal* MARIAN, *in the light of the torch, mud-spattered with her coat ripped, and scratch marks on her face*]

[*She makes straight for the kitchen to wash her face and hands, while he re-bolts and re-locks the two doors*]

Lenny	Are you hurt bad?
Marian	Scratched a bit, but not as much as my car is.
Lenny	You found it?
Marian	It's the centrepiece of the barricade at the entrance to the estate up there.
Lenny	I suppose it's where we should have looked first.
Marian	There wasn't anybody about, I tried to drive it away.
Lenny	Chrissake, Marian, that was totally asking for it!
Marian	They knew me instantly on sight of course – "that fenian hoor of a squatter" – that's what they actually think we are – squatters.

Lenny	Right.
Marian	It's quite funny, actually.
Lenny	That's it. We're moving out.
Marian	It was all women – shrieking and squealing and scrabbing at me, is that your radio? [*She has just spotted it on the table*]
Lenny	We can camp out in my place . . .
Marian	I thought I told you to keep it out of here. [*Thrusting the radio into his midriff*]
Lenny	Where's Ruth and Peter? [*Registering the radio*] Whose is this?
Marian	Yeah, take him and her with you both. If you walk across town you should have no problems.
Lenny	We'll leave together, all four of us.
Marian	I'm the one who lives here, if you recall. I'm going nowhere, I've only just got home.
Lenny	Marian, we're not talking personal issues, not any longer. This right here is Nazi Belfast now, and it's us playing the Jews.
Marian	God, but you're simple. People, cast adrift, in hysterics . . . spare me your vision of the Third Reich in Ballyhackamore.
Lenny	Look at yourself. Look at the news. It's nearly two weeks now, the animals have taken over the zoo, it's all poised on the verge of a massive pogrom, we're sitting here like a row of ducks in a shooting gallery.
	[MARIAN *has been getting out a big church candle from a drawer and lighting it, to supplement the light from the camping lamp left behind by* RUTH *and* PETER]
Marian	Sounds to me like you haven't got a minute to lose.
Lenny	Right, okay. I'm withdrawing the house from sale.
Marian	Ruth's car is still sitting up there, untouched, up in the churchyard, if you want to try using that. You better go and get your gear together, there's a good boy.
Lenny	The contracts are off. Null and void.
Marian	Yes, well away you and explain all that to your Uncle Phelim, if you can track him down in his underground bunker, it's somewhere up Fortwilliam way, isn't that right?

Lenny	What exactly do you envisage happening here – the National Trust turning up in riot gear and storming the house to rescue you?
Marian	I'm seeing this through. That's all. On my own terms. For Jesus' sake just leave me in peace, the whole shower of you, I'm sick of your filth and mess and noise and bickering, in every last corner of the house, I've had enough.
Lenny	Marian . . .
Marian	You find a refuge, you find a task for your life, and then wholesale panic breaks out, and they all come crowding in the door, her and you and that trend-worshipping narcissist . . .
Lenny	It's beside the point, you're in terrible danger, we've all got to get out of here. The last thing I ever intended or needed, me and you under the same roof, it was another one of his lame jokes, [*Gesturing skywards*] okay, we move out, we go our separate ways to our respective families. I don't like to see you in the state you're in. You're just not fit to be left on your own.
	[MARIAN *slowly turns on him*]
Marian	What are you getting at?
Lenny	I'm talking about what's going on!
Marian	Such as?
Lenny	What have we been having this entire conversation about?
Marian	You consider that I'm cracking up?
Lenny	When did I say that?
Marian	Not fit to be alone?
Lenny	In this house, that's all!
Marian	It wouldn't maybe have occurred to you, it wouldn't maybe have penetrated even that dim featherweight brain – that being on my own is the one thing I am fit for?
Lenny	Okay . . .
Marian	That being on my own is precisely what I bought this house for, the reason I sold my business and my flat, the reason I reconciled myself to meeting you for an evening to look this place over?
Lenny	Okay, okay, but it's all changed – out there!

Marian	It's all changed in here, Lenny. For five weeks you've been living with me again. It took me three years to break out of our marriage, and now for the past five weeks you've been living with me again, here in this house, the very place I chose as a refuge. So even if you do believe that I'm cracking up . . .
Lenny	I never said you were cracking up . . .
Marian	. . . it's conceivably not actually a psychiatrist that I need . . .
Lenny	Who said you needed a psychiatrist?
Marian	You've always been very ready with that solution in the past.
Lenny	For pity's sake, Marian . . .
Marian	It may just be that all I need is to get the three spineless parasites, with whom I'm presently saddled, off my back – or maybe your uncle the psychiatrist would consider such a desire irrational?
Lenny	Quit it, will you, just scrub it, it's the same old trick all over, putting words into my mouth to avoid facing your own reality . . .
Marian	Don't start the usual bloody put-upon whinge, I'm not one of your doting maiden aunts, I can see clean through it, you can't face up to emotion in any shape or form . . .
Lenny	Here it comes.
Marian	Feeling. Passion. This. [*Jabbing at her heart*] Every time I stubbed my toe or smashed a tumbler and swore loudly, you were offering to turn me over to your uncle the psychiatrist, it's beyond your capability, grown-up anger, pain, commitment, love – have you never considered that if one of us needs treatment it might be you?
Lenny	I never know how you do this, I start off trying to help you, and within ten minutes I'm a villain, I'm a deviant, I'm the one in need of help, in the name of God just face reality!
Marian	Which reality did you have in mind?
Lenny	Your own, Marian, your own reality, you've been talking to yourself, you've been counting spoons, you've been babbling in tongues in the middle of the night!
	[*Too late he realises the blunder. Now that she has successfully accomplished it, Marian relaxes*]
Marian	Thanks, Lenny. Very much. I thought we were never going to get to it.

Lenny	Well, what are we <u>supposed</u> to think?
Marian	Don't think, Lenny. Don't think anything at all. Don't even try. It doesn't agree with you. Here's what we're doing. I'm staying here with my tongues – and you're going home with your trombone. That way we're all quits. Okay?
Lenny	I don't know why I waste my time. You'd think I'd know better by now.

[*He retires, out the hall door and back up the stairs*]

[MARIAN *closes the door after him*]

[LILY MATTHEWS *immediately appears from the shadows of the pantry. She is wearing the print dress now without the pinafore over it, and her hair is down: we can see in her the ghost of her 33-year-old self*]

Lily	Nice way to treat your own husband.
Marian	Lenny's no husband of anybody's. Never was, never will be.
Lily	In the eyes of God he's your man still.
Marian	God's eyes were put out, Lily, did you not hear.
Lily	What sort of talk is that?
Marian	The old boy. Blinded. He only exists in the dark now.
Lily	Have you drink taken?
Marian	We're his guide dogs now. Dragging him round from pillar to post. Half of us in rut, and the other half rabid. Without us, he can't survive. But without him, without him, to love, honour and obey . . . it's just a dog's life for us. So far as I can see.
Lily	Is this the sort of blasphemous babble the priests are filling your heads with now?
Marian	What makes you think I'm a Catholic?
Lily	I suppose that's your idea of amusement. Sacrilege and mockery.
Marian	You're out in your figure today, I see. Where did you get that dress from, anyway?
Lily	Mind your own business.
Marian	The height of the Depression, Alfie two years jobless . . . it was Alan Ferris bought it for you, wasn't it.
Lily	What if it was, he was a good lodger and a good friend to us.

Marian	The English airman. Stores and maintenance, Sydenham aerodrome.
Lily	It was only him spied it, that was the reason. Hanging in Price's window. He egged me on to try it on for size, it was my birthday, that was why. Before I know where I am, he's the money out and paid across the counter, and me walking out of the shop still wearing it. When he was in one of those daft oul' moods of his, he could charm the birds down out of the trees.
Marian	Crêpe-de-chine.
Lily	I never owned anything like that in my life before, the sheer clean feel of it all over you . . .
Marian	Did you go dancing?
Lily	I was a married woman of thirty-three, catch yourself on.
Marian	You went to Groomsport, though.
Lily	Who told you that?
Marian	I'm thirty-three as well, Lily.
Lily	What of it?
Marian	Did you make a day of it?
Lily	No, we did not, his skin was very fair, he burnt easy, he didn't like the sand. It was only an evening dander along the front. The sun was setting over the lough, hanging out of the sky like a big swollen blood orange. The water all glistening with the redness of it and the sky and the hills on fire with it. Like what you'd see after a war, maybe . . . it took your breath away, it was a real picture, but it was frightening. That's what I thought anyhow.
Marian	Did you say it?
Lily	He laughed. Nothing frightened him.
Marian	Why would it.
Lily	We stood there and looked, at the water, and the air. He'd come from across the water, you see. Flown across, through the air. I'd never even been on the water, let alone up in the air, couldn't imagine it. I wanted to. It was frightening, but. We just stood there and looked, in the cool of the evening, drinking it in.
Marian	I could do with an evening in Groomsport myself, just at the minute.

[*She sits down in the rocking chair*]

Lily   All we did was stand and look, across the water.

Marian   That was the moment when it hit you, though. You already could tell that he wanted you. That was the moment you realised that you were going to give yourself . . . all of yourself, whatever he wanted to do to you, that same evening . . .

Lily   Keep you your guttersnipe mind to yourself, what do you know about my life, over forty years ago!

Marian   Only what I've read, Lily.

[*She reaches into the raffia basket which is tucked in beside the rocking chair, and takes out an old and disintegrating leather-bound padlocked diary*]

Lily   How did you get hold of that?

Marian   Under the cellar stairs wasn't the ideal place for it. There's dampness there. Mildew. Rust. The lock has rusted away, look.

[*She holds up the diary and it swings open, the lock coming adrift*]

Lily   Leave that be, that's private property, don't you dare touch that!

Marian   You wanted it read, Lily, you must have.

Lily   No!

Marian   Why else hide it? Why write it? You wanted somebody to know. It's just turned out to be me, that's all.

Lily   Why can't you mind your own business, what right have you to go poking and prying into a body's private life . . .

Marian   What about the life of your baby?

Lily   My baby was strong . . . he was well happed-up . . .

Marian   You abandoned him.

Lily   I entrusted him to the care of the Lord!

Marian   You left him lying in the porch of a Baptist church!

Lily   A well-off congregation, it was for the best . . . moneyed people . . . some pair of them would take him in, adopt him as their own, what did you want me to do, he had a better chance there than the orphanage or the hospital . . .

Marian   He would have had his best chance right here, being reared by
               you and Alfie.

Lily   My Alfie would have struck the pair of us down dead. He was
               capable of it, he knew it too, he told me the day we moved
               in here, never make me lose my temper . . . he never found
               out, about the child, that was the one mercy, he was away
               that whole year tramping all over England, looking for work
               with Jackie Midgely. Nobody ever knew but me, my own
               mother was dead by then with the T.B., I was inclined towards
               stoutness then anyway . . . one day it just arrived . . . on that
               floor, five hours I lay there . . . I delivered it myself. By the
               time Alfie come home again, the whole thing was over and
               done, as though it had never been . . . he had no inkling of any
               of it, from then till his dying day.

Marian   You and Alan Ferris. On the front parlour sofa. He'd no
               inkling of that?

Lily   Oh, sweet God in heaven forgive me!

Marian   Alfie was impotent, wasn't he. A souvenir of Passchendaele,
               maybe. Scarcely the first nor the last to come back from the
               dead in that condition.

Lily   I sinned against my own flesh in lust and fornication, I had to
               desert my own baby, nobody ever knew only the Lord our
               God knew and His eye was on me all right, burning into the
               very soul of me, He alone was witness to the torment that
               I've suffered every living hour in this house where the very
               walls and doors cry out against me, there was never anybody
               to tell the knife that went through me a dozen dozen times
               a day, minding how I left my child, walking away from him,
               leaving him bundled up there in that wooden box, nobody
               to help me, only me here in this house, gnawing and tearing
               away at my own heart and lights, day in day out . . . until I was
               all consumed by my own wickedness, on the inside, nothing
               left but the shell of me, for appearance's sake . . . still and all.
               At least I never let myself down – never cracked. Never
               surrendered. Not one inch. I went to my grave a respectable
               woman, Mrs Alfred George Matthews, I never betrayed him.
               That was the way I atoned, you see. I done him proud. He
               never knew any reason to be ashamed of me, or doubt my
               loyalty. From the day we met till the day I went to my grave.

Marian   You loved Alan Ferris, Lily. These things can't be helped. He
               introduced you to the body's actual passion. The English
               airman. Then he flew away.

Lily

Alan . . . he came from across the water, you see . . . there was a picture in my Bible, at Sunday school, the fair-skinned archangel standing at the gates of heaven, that was what he looked like . . . only he was a dark angel. Angel of death. Agent of Satan. He swept me up, high up, took me up into the sky . . . and then he dropped me. Left me. Flew home. Left me falling. Falling.

[MARIAN *takes* LILY's *hand and holds it against her own heart*]

Marian

Forgive me, Lily.

[*Lights fade to blackout*]

[*End of Scene Four*]

V

[*The early hours of Sunday, June 2nd*]

[MARIAN *is asleep on the sofa in the dark kitchen. There is a glimmering of distant bonfires in the night sky above the yard, and the faint sounds of an Orange band playing and of a mob celebrating*]

[*Gradually this is overtaken by the din of a military helicopter approaching and hovering low over the house*]

[PETER *appears outside, dragging himself up on to the top of the yard wall, having climbed up from a dustbin in the alley on the far side. He has a banjo case slung across his back*]

[*He is suddenly caught in the blinding searchlight of the hovering helicopter. He shields his eyes from the light with an arm*]

[MARIAN, *awakened by this, goes to the window.* PETER *drops down into the yard and makes for the scullery door.* MARIAN *goes to it and lets him in. The searchlight switches off and the helicopter moves away*]

[MARIAN *is lighting the gas mantles as* PETER *talks*]

Peter   Couldn't get back into the street . . . just young bloods drunk, dozens of them, hooligan types, I was carrying a couple of bottles, you see, they probably thought it was whiskey or something, they'd a shock in store, it was my father's elderberry wine. You wouldn't exactly want to die for it, Christ . . . I'm all slashed on that wall. At least I managed to hang on to my old banjo. Cold, isn't it. Sorry to disturb you. I hadn't expected, what with the strike being over, I see the gas supply has returned anyway . . .

Marian   Not to mention the Army.

Peter   What? Oh, right, right, the chopper, yeah, I was actually bloody glad, as a matter of fact, it showing up, at least it got them off my back . . .

Marian   There's a glimmer of life in that fire. Hoke it out and throw those sticks on it.

[*She exits to the bathroom to fetch the first-aid kit.* PETER, *alone and shivering, goes to the press where the remains of the drink are stored and takes a swig of vodka*]

[RUTH *rushes in, in her nightdress*]

Ruth	Marian says you were attacked . . .
Peter	I'm fine.
Ruth	You poor love, you're all cut . . .

[PETER *thrusts his bloodstained hand in front of her face*]

Peter	Oh yeah, the red hand. Makes you puke, doesn't it. Blood and things.

[*He turns away from her and tends to the fire*]

Ruth	I'm only trying to be your friend, Peter.

[MARIAN *returns with Lily's first-aid box*]

Peter	I'll let you both get back to sleep, then.
Marian	Sit down.
Peter	I'll just go and get myself cleaned up . . . [*But she has firmly planted him in the chair and is starting to swab the cuts on his hands*] . . . ah. Well. Thanks. Funny time for this, isn't it. They're all celebrating, out there. My crowd and hers, I mean. The end of being forced to share the top table with a few Popeheads, they're beside themselves with the glorious deliverance of it, the executive forced to resign, you'd think they'd given birth, actually created something for once, instead of battering it to death, yet again, the only kind of victory they ever credit, holding the good old fort, stamping the life out of anything that starts to creep forward, even my reverend father and mother were quietly crowing over it, in the same way she is of course, [*At* RUTH] with a proper air of restrained well-balanced smugness . . .
Ruth	Stop it!
Peter	What odds, they're all one, under the skin, all at one with those vicious little buggers, out there, who put their toecaps into me . . . [*He suddenly breaks down but immediately swallows it back*] . . . sorry, I don't know . . .
Marian	It's this stuff, it shows no mercy.
Peter	I don't, I don't know why it matters, why I care, I don't know, what the fuck I have to come back here for, what I expect, what it is I think I'll find here, whatever it is I think I'm missing . . .

[LENNY *comes in from the hall, returning from a gig, in his street clothes, and carrying his trombone*]

Lenny	What's going on, then?
Ruth	Peter got roughed up.

[*She brushes out past him*]

Lenny	[*To* PETER] I thought you were visiting your parents?
Peter	Correct.
Lenny	What happened?
Peter	Who knows – my mother just suddenly went for my hands with a broken bottle.
Lenny	Your mother's a justice of the peace!

[MARIAN *is finishing cleaning the cuts on* PETER's *hands and putting plaster on them*]

Peter	[*To* MARIAN] Did he ever tell you how close we came to preventing the entire Ulster conflict from getting off the ground?
Marian	Bound to have.
Lenny	You're not referring to McManus, I hope?
Marian	Bound to be.

[RUTH *re-enters wearing a dressing gown*]

Peter	There was a spaceman we all knew, as students, you see, Ruth – a wild mad bugger called Vincent Moog McManus, he stayed on indefinitely as a research student in Chemistry. [LENNY *has retreated to the kitchen to fetch himself a scrap of food*] He spent most of his time in the lab synthesizing LSD – the drug, that is – and I'm not talking in spoonfuls, he had rows of big sweety jars lined along his kitchen shelves, chocolate eclairs, liquorice comfits, you name it, all fully primed. This was high-class stuff, before anybody here had even heard tell of it, Moog was a bona-fide visionary. So one hot night, pinhead here and me and Moog were tripped out in my garden, beatific, except there'd been the early riots, the initial killings, the first stirrings of the reawakening of the Protestant dragon and the Catholic dragon, and the three of us felt a messianic impulse, to slay these ancient monsters, we felt summoned, as a holy trinity of the new age, father son and holy ghost, Moog being the ghost and me the messiah, but it was Godhead here who came up with the redemption – why not take the total stash of acid in Moog's sweety jars, transport it up to the Mourne

Mountains, and dump it into the Silent Valley reservoir? The entire Belfast water supply was in that lovely man-made lake. We could turn on the population, comprehensively, with one simple transcendental gesture, that would be it, the doors of perception flung wide, wholesale mind-shift, no more bigotry and hatred, a city full of spaced-out contemplatives like the three of us.

So off I went and filched the keys of my mother's Austin Princess, and we loaded it up with the sweety jars and headed for the hills. We actually got as far as Dundrum . . . before negative signals began to filter through even to us, scrambled brains and all, we hadn't seen the news, not for days, that was the basic flaw. The Silent Valley reservoir had been blown up by the U.V.F. Belfast was dry. The Mourne Mountains were swarming like an anthill with the security forces. We got searched three times on the way home . . . Moog said he was a supplier for his family's confectionery business, it was true in a way, not that it made any odds, they wouldn't have known the drug if we'd force-fed them on it, we were entirely beside the point, am I right, head? What the hell. At least we tried. How many can say as much.

[LENNY *has registered the banjo*]

Lenny   Is that your old five-string?

Peter   Haven't played it in five years.

Lenny   How's the tuning?

Peter   You tell me.

[LENNY *removes the banjo from its case and quietly tunes it up during the ensuing dialogue*]

Peter   So anyway, there you go. That's my bedtime story. Time for you three girls to kiss and tell. Seeing as we're all up and about. What do you say, Marian? How about dishing the real dirt on Orange Lily Matthews, you must have dug up some scandal by this time.

Marian   I found a used condom behind the parlour sofa. [*An awkward moment all round*] The pair of you might have cleaned up behind you, at least.

Peter   I don't think much of that, as a story.

Ruth   I really am sorry, Marian . . .

Marian	I'll give you a story. Lily sat in that parlour, right through the Blitz. Alfie was a fire warden, out most nights – she promised him she'd stay down in the cellar during the air-raids, instead of which she sat up in that front parlour, in the blackout, the pitch dark, listening to the war in the air . . . the bombers and the fighters, the ack-ack and the shells falling, falling and exploding . . . she stretched out on that self-same sofa, where Alan Ferris had stretched her out seven years earlier and pleasured her till her ears sang with a whole wild uncontainable babble . . .
Peter	Holy shit, tell us more.
Lenny	Quiet.
Marian	She lay down in the dark on her own now, and pictured him, up there, burning a hole through the sky, a dark angel, and her ears roared now with the rage of a wholesale slaughter, pounding the ground under her and the air all round her, armageddon, random and blind, pulverising her whole body until she once more came and came again, and she composed herself to die there, waiting for the chosen bomb to fall on her and cleanse her terrible sinfulness and shame . . . the street next to this one was totally flattened one night. The parlour windows came in on her, but Lily wasn't even scratched. The skies cleared. The war ended. And there she still was – unscathed. She interpreted this as her punishment. She had been condemned to life. A life sentence.
	[*They are all reduced to silence, staring into the fire*]
Lenny	I wonder what it was like here. Before Christianity.
Ruth	What are you going to do with the house, Marian?
Marian	Live in it.
Peter	National Trust permitting, you mean.
Marian	That was a wrong impulse. A mistaken idea. It would only have been perpetuating a crime . . . condemning her to life indefinitely. I'm clearing most of this out. Keeping just the basics. Fixing it up. What this house needs most is air and light.
	[*She starts building up the fire with turf*]
Peter	Exactly what I say. Minor gentrification. [*To* LENNY] As for you, head, you appear to be saying nothing.
Lenny	What of it?

Peter	It's your turn for the story.
Lenny	[*Offering him the banjo*] Here, you're in tune now.
Peter	You play it, I think I've lost my touch. [*Holding up his hands*] Give us a talking blues.

[LENNY *fools around on the banjo for a moment*]

Lenny   There was something happened to me last summer – as it happens – last August, down near Kinsale. [*He sets the banjo aside*] There's a Dutch guy with a pub there, runs a lot of jazz nights. This particular night went on till half-six in the morning, the sun was hanging out, I was ready for a look at the ocean, so was the lady vocalist. She was a strange woman, half gipsy, from Sligo or somewhere weird like that, totally wrecked on everything on offer, which was plenty . . . so. We stumbled down to this cove, a lovely horseshoe of sand, except her and me couldn't handle any more bright lights, so we collapsed on to a sheltered bit of grass behind some boulders. And your woman starts crooning. [*Sings*] "Just a closer walk with thee . . . " lying there splayed out in the warm singing away . . . and she begins to peel her clothes off. Nothing to do with me – she was stretched out flat with her eyes closed – but before too long, she's entirely bare, the voice floating in the early breeze, [*Sings*] "Grant it Jesus if you please . . . " and I'm hunkered down beside her, with a swollen mouth from playing all night, staring out at the glittery water, stunned all over, the way you are. And then, into my line of vision – there comes this sight, at first I thought I was hallucinating, it was a gaggle of nuns, real nuns, in the whole gear, which they were busy stripping off, over their heads. There was a dozen or more of them. It was a nuns' swimming party. Underneath their habits, they had these interlock jobs, sort of vests and baggy long johns. I suppose they reckoned at that hour there'd be nobody to see them. So down they pelted into the sea, frisking around and frolicking like nine-year-olds, the noise of it – while your woman is meanwhile stretched out starkers beside me, singing this deep-throated heartfelt version of "Just a Closer Walk With Thee" . . . entirely oblivious . . . and the nuns are splashing each other, and giggling and screaming, and flinging themselves about in the golden light, with the wet interlock clinging to their excited bodies – and it doesn't take a lot to see that the nuns are experiencing their sex and the vocalist her spirit. And for a crazy few seconds I all but sprinted down to the nuns to churn

	my body into theirs, in the surf foam, and then bring them all back to the lady vocalist, for a session of great spirituals . . . and maybe that's how it was . . . what it was like here. Before Christianity. Is what I'm saying.
Ruth	You don't even know Christianity. You think it's only denial, but that's wrong. It's meant to be love and celebration. You don't even know what day it is now, the meaning of it.
Peter	You tell them, Ruthie child. Pentecost Sunday.
Lenny	So what? [*He has turned away from this to his trombone, which he takes out and cleans and puts together*]
Ruth	The day our Lord's apostles were inspired by the Holy Spirit. "And when the day of Pentecost was fully come, they were all with one accord in one place. And suddenly there came a sound from heaven as of a rushing mighty wind, and it filled all the house where they were sitting. And there appeared unto them cloven tongues like as of fire, and it sat upon each of them. And they were all filled with the Holy Ghost, and began to speak with other tongues, as the Spirit gave them utterance."
	[*She retreats into herself again*]
Peter	You can't stop there. It's your story, you have to finish it.
Ruth	I don't remember it all.
Peter	"And they were all amazed, and were in doubt, saying to one another, What meaneth this? . . . "
Ruth	"Others mocking said, These men are full of new wine . . . "
Peter	"But Peter, standing up with the eleven, lifted up his voice and said unto them: Ye men of Judea and all ye that dwell at Jerusalem, let this be known unto you and hearken to my words: For these are not drunken as ye suppose, seeing it is but the third hour of the day . . . "
Ruth	[*Squaring up to him, as it turns into a contest*] "But this is that which was spoken by the prophet Joel: And it shall come to pass in the last days, saith God, I will pour out of my spirit upon all flesh: and your sons and your daughters shall prophesy, and your young men shall see visions, and your old men shall dream dreams. And on my servants and on my handmaidens I will pour out in those days of my spirit; and they shall prophesy . . . "

Peter	"And I will shew wonders in heaven above, and signs in the earth beneath; blood and fire, and vapour of smoke; the sun shall be turned into darkness, and the moon into blood, before that great and notable day of the Lord come . . . "
Ruth	"And it shall come to pass, that whosoever shall call on the name of the Lord shall be saved."
Peter	The old familiar payoff! — but it hasn't entirely held up, Ruthie. I mean they're never done calling on the name of the Lord in this wee province of ours, so it ought to be the most saved place on God's earth instead of the most absolutely godforsaken, not so?
Ruth	Some of us love this province.
Peter	By God you do and with a vengeance, and you've finally loved it to death, Ruth, stone dead and in its grave and we're all sitting here at the wake. Take a long hard look. Because our whole wee family's here, gathered together round the hearth, our <u>holy</u> family — Marian the mother at the head, the holy virgin, shielding us from all harm, keeping faithful little Ruthie safe from her night fears, the funny-coloured buses and the psychopathic Christian spouse . . .
Ruth	Leave you David out of this, you're not worth a hair of his head!
Peter	We're certainly not in any doubt that you'll be going back to him.
Ruth	He's up in Purdysburn Hospital, if you must know.
Marian	What happened?
Ruth	He's had a breakdown. Smashed his own two hands to a pulp before they could restrain him.
Marian	You never told me, Ruth.
Ruth	I went to visit him. Told him it was over. He's accepted it. He knows I won't be going back.
Peter	Why not? I thought you were hell-bent on being a nurse.
Lenny	All right, enough! No more.
Marian	Leave him. Let him get rid of it.
Peter	You see how she forgives the one stray sheep, the prodigal, we're such an Irish little family, the strong saintly suffering ma and the shiftless clown of a da here, no damn use to man or

beast, hunched up against the wall, hands in empty pockets, jiggling his limp thing like a dead hen's thrapple . . .

Lenny   No more of this shit tonight . . .

[PETER *grabs hold of him*]

Peter   Pentecost is upon us, head, so where's the fire on your tongue? Or is there maybe not a fizzle left in any part of you at all?

Lenny   Not like you, I suppose, dicking your way round the Brummie discos every night of the week . . .

Peter   You're never going to leave here, face it, your life's locked in and the key surrendered . . .

Lenny   I'll live whatever life I choose, and I'll live it here, what's it to you, you think you're any further on? You seriously think I'd want what you have? I live like a prince compared to you, I live for my real friends, for good crack, I'm a musician, I live for what I play!

Peter   On that? [*The trombone*] Play on that? You want to know what playing on that is? Farting into the wind.

[LENNY, *with a sudden spasm of rage, dislogdges* PETER*'s grip on him, flings him across the table, and then turns away in self-disgust*]

Peter   [*Winded, picking himself up*] Of course . . . we're null and void as a holy family, aren't we . . . missing our most important member . . . the Prince of Peace Himself. [*Pulling himself painfully into a seat*] Can you see him? Here? Can you see him? Dandering down Royal Avenue? Dropping into a Council meeting at the City Hall? The Son of Man . . . in the middle of the marching ranks of the Ulster zealots, watching at the elbow of the holy Catholic Nationalist zealot as he puts a pistol to a man's knee, to a man's brains, to a man's balls, the Son of God in the polling booth, observing the votes being cast in support of that, suffering the little children with murder festering in their hearts, what would Jesus Holy Christ do with us all here, would you say?

Lenny   I'll tell you exactly what he'd do, he'd close down every church and chapel, temple and tabernacle in the whole island, put them to the torch, burn them into rubble, turf the congregations out priests and pastors face first, and drive them up into the mountains, up to the boniest, bleakest stretches of the Sperrins and the Mournes, and he'd flay them into the rock, until the Christianity was scourged out of the

very marrows of their bones, he'd expunge religion once
and for all from off the face of this country, until the people
could discover no mercy except in each other, no belief
except to believe in each other, no forgiveness but what the
other would forgive, until they cried out in the dark for each
other and embraced their own humanity . . . that's the only
redemption he'd offer them. Never mind believing in Jesus
Christ. That's the point at which Jesus Christ might just begin
to believe in us.

Peter   Why would he come near the place, let's face it, he's already
been crucified once. He's already been once in hell.

Lenny   The Church invented hell. They've just used this town to
show us what they mean.

Marian   They. They. You think you can both shuffle it off, so easily,
with your righteous anger, let me tell you, you're not even
in the same league as I am for righteous anger, I've supped
on precious little else for five years past, it changes nothing.
Forget the church. Forget the priests and pastors. There is
some kind of christ, in every one of us. [PETER *and* LENNY *turn
their faces against this language*] Each of us either honours him,
or denies him and violates him, what we do to him is done to
ourselves. I had a child once.

Lenny   No. Marian . . .

Marian   I called him Christopher. Because he was a kind of Christ to
me, he brought love with him . . . the truth and the life. He was
a future. Until one day I found him dead. I thought like you
for a long time. He chose death in the cot rather than life in
this town, in these times, it was their fault, they had done it
to me, I hated them. Hated life. It was all a lie, of course. The
cause and effect were in me, in him too, [*At* LENNY] we were
mortal after all, we were human, had to be, we couldn't bear
one another, couldn't tolerate ourselves, the child was only a
fallible mortal the same as us, that was all that he was telling
us. I felt him as a raw scar across my own spirit, stinging
me, every minute, every hour, everything defaced by it . . .
until I was blaming him, for all the pain, he was one of them
too. They. I denied him. The christ in him. Which he had
entrusted to my care, the ghost of him that I do still carry,
as I carried his little body. The christ in him absorbed into
the christ in me. We have got to love that in ourselves.
In ourselves first and then in them. That's the only future
there is.

[*She has been on her feet during this, and is close to the sofa where* LENNY *is sitting, hunched up, close to tears now. Privately and unobtrusively, he touches her hand*]

Personally, I want to live now. I want this house to live. We have committed sacrilege enough on life, in this place, in these times. We don't just owe it to ourselves, we owe it to our dead too . . . our innocent dead. They're not our masters, they're only our creditors, for the life they never knew. We owe them at least that – the fullest life for which they could ever have hoped, we carry those ghosts within us, to betray those hopes is the real sin against the christ, and I for one cannot commit it one day longer.

[*The sky above the backyard has been growing light*]

[LENNY, *overwhelmed by what* MARIAN *has said, picks up his trombone and goes out to the backyard. He sits down on the window ledge*]

[RUTH, *at the table, opens her Bible at the second chapter of the Acts of the Apostles. She reads from it*]

Ruth   "Therefore did my heart rejoice, and my tongue was glad; moreover also my flesh shall rest in hope: Because thou wilt not leave my soul in hell, neither wilt thou suffer thine Holy One to see corruption. Thou hast made known to me the ways of life; thou shalt make me full of joy with thy countenance."

[*During this,* LENNY *has started to play a very slow and soulful version of "Just a Closer Walk with Thee"*]

[*After some time,* PETER *picks up his banjo from where it has been left lying, close to him. Tentatively, he starts to pick out an accompaniment to the tune*]

[RUTH *reaches across and opens the window*]

[*As the music swells, the lights fade, very slowly, to blackout*]

[*The End*]